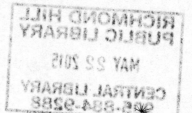

THE 3 PROMISES

FIND JOY EVERY DAY.
DO WHAT YOU LOVE.
MAKE A DIFFERENCE.

DAVID J. POLLAY

STERLING
New York

STERLING
New York

An Imprint of Sterling Publishing
387 Park Avenue South
New York, NY 10016

STERLING and the distinctive Sterling logo are registered trademarks
of Sterling Publishing Co., Inc.

ISBN 978-1-4549-1248-4

Distributed in Canada by Sterling Publishing
c/o Canadian Manda Group, 165 Dufferin Street
Toronto, Ontario, Canada M6K 3H6
Distributed in the United Kingdom by GMC Distribution Services
Castle Place, 166 High Street, Lewes, East Sussex, England BN7 1XU
Distributed in Australia by Capricorn Link (Australia) Pty. Ltd.
P.O. Box 704, Windsor, NSW 2756, Australia

For information about custom editions, special sales, and premium and corporate purchases,
please contact Sterling Special Sales at 800-805-5489 or specialsales@sterlingpublishing.com.

Manufactured in the United States of America

2 4 6 8 10 9 7 5 3 1

www.sterlingpublishing.com

Interior design by Christine Heun
Original cover design by Katie Otis
Sterling cover design by David Ter-Avanesyon

For Dawn, Eliana, and Ariela
For Jerriann and Louis
For Mike

Contents

PART THREE

Make A Difference: The Third Promise

PART FOUR

THE 3 PROMISES CHALLENGE

PART FIVE

AMPLIFY YOUR POSITIVE IMPACT

The 3 Promises Revealed

"Promises are the uniquely human way of ordering the future, making it
predictable and reliable to the extent that this is humanly possible."
—Hannah Arendt

I'VE UNCOVERED THE PATH TO FULFILLMENT—A WHOLE NEW WAY OF LIVING
that gives you sustainable joy, career satisfaction, and the power to make
a difference in other people's lives, simply by making these three daily
promises to yourself.

Find Joy Every Day.

Do What You Love.

Make a Difference.

When I meet people who are genuinely thoughtful about their lives, many
admit to feeling somewhat resigned to not having as much happiness,
meaningful work, and connections with others as they might wish. Do you
want your life to be as richly fulfilling as your dreams but doubt your ability
and means to accomplish this?

I'm here to tell you that your dreams are within your grasp—and you
don't have to settle for anything less. I want you to be happy now and to
commit today to building the life you want for the future. You can live an
extraordinary life. My mission is to show you how to craft and experience a
fulfilling life every day.

More Than Happy

WHEN I UNCOVERED THE 3 PROMISES, I REALIZED SOMETHING: FEELING unhappy felt bad, but feeling unfulfilled felt even worse. It's one thing to feel unhappy, but it's a lot worse to feel that you're squandering your natural strengths, wasting opportunities to help others, and missing times to be joyful with the people you love and care about. But it doesn't have to be this way. After years of practicing positive psychology in major corporations and with people from more than 100 countries, I have learned that engaging in fulfilling activities on a *daily* basis is what truly leads to happiness.

Do the things that bring you joy. Happiness will come.

Do the things that you love to do. Happiness will come.

Do the things that make a difference to others.

Happiness will come.

When you live a fulfilling life, you will be happy. That's awesome news, because it means that you are not locked into a limited, predetermined amount of happiness, either by your genes or the constraints of the past. It means you're not at the mercy of other people's moods, attitudes, and behaviors (or your own, for that matter), and you're not the victim of circumstances. It means you're free . . . free to live a fulfilling life. "When," you might ask? The answer is "now!"

Your Fulfillment

SO MANY OF US GET LOST IN OTHER PEOPLE'S OPINIONS ABOUT WHAT fulfillment is, or is not, and get confused by the lack of agreement on the criteria we should use to measure it. This lack of clarity can leave us feeling dissatisfied, anxious, or depressed.

When you look back at previous weeks and tease out the days, can you say which ones were happy? If it takes an effort to remember, or if you're simply not sure what you were feeling, you're not alone: Most of us do not have a clear idea of what makes up a happy day or a happy life. If your definition of fulfillment is based on securing a better job, a more supportive spouse, better health, friendlier neighbors, or more cooperative co-workers, these criteria might make it harder, and take longer, to attain your dream of a happier, more fulfilled life.

The good news is that achieving fulfillment does not need to be a laborious process that takes a lifetime to complete, nor does it boil down unrealistically to feeling happy all day long.

Fulfillment is finding joy in your day, every day. No matter your situation, you deserve a smile, a laugh, a hug—a simple break from the day's demands and responsibilities. Fulfillment is about doing something that expresses what you love to do each day—the thing you're most passionate about—through your work, your relationships, your hobbies.

And you don't have to quit your job and leave your family for a year to search for your purpose in life. Fulfillment is about making a difference every day—consciously thinking of opportunities beyond your immediate self-interest to give to others.

Your Story

NO MATTER WHAT YOUR CIRCUMSTANCES ARE, I WANT THE STORY YOU TELL yourself and others to be one of fulfillment. I want your life story to be one of joy, self-expression, and contribution.

Life can be hard. You will face disappointment, disease, and death at some point; at other times you may feel discouragement, depression, or despair. You can try to mask what makes you sad, angry, and hurt, but you cannot remove these feelings from your life—the reality is that they'll come and go as events occur in your life.

But through it all, your life has a distinct story line. As I am writing this book, you are living your story. You are interpreting events in your past, situations in the present, and possibilities in the future. Your story guides your actions every day, and it influences others every day. Knowing that your story is not fixed and is written anew every day, I have a bold ambition for you and a big request: I ask you to look at your life through the lens of the 3 Promises in order to Find Joy Every Day, Do What You Love, and Make a Difference.

This book is about your fulfillment at home, at work, and in your community. It's about the good life you deserve. It's your encouragement to live a fulfilling life now. Not later in the year. Not tomorrow. Starting today.

This book is for you when times are good and when life is hard. It's here to help you make the 3 Promises and keep them.

Thank you for joining me on this journey. I'm grateful you're with me.

—David J. Pollay

The 3 Promises Quiz

BEFORE YOUR JOURNEY GETS FULLY UNDERWAY, LET'S SEE HOW COMPLETELY you are living the 3 Promises today. How fulfilled are you? The 3 Promises Quiz will help you establish your baseline and shine a light on the opportunities you have to create more joy, passion, and meaning in your life. So let's get started. Circle your answers below.

Do you Find Joy every day?

1 = Never | 2 = Seldom | 3 = About Half the time | 4 = Usually | 5 = Always

Do you Do What You Love every day?

1 = Never | 2 = Seldom | 3 = About Half the time | 4 = Usually | 5 = Always

Do you Make a Difference every day?

1 = Never | 2 = Seldom | 3 = About Half the time | 4 = Usually | 5 = Always

Add your scores from the three questions above. Write your total score in the box below.

Your Total 3 Promises Fulfillment Score:

The Key

LOCATE YOUR SCORE BELOW TO FIND OUT HOW FULFILLED YOU ARE ON A daily basis.

A SCORE BETWEEN 10 AND 15 INDICATES THAT YOU ARE LIVING A complete, or nearly complete, life of fulfillment. No matter the circumstances in your life, you still manage to Find Joy Every Day, Do What You Love, and Make a Difference. You have difficult days and disappointments, but they do not crowd out your joy, passion, and meaningful life. By living the 3 Promises, you successfully navigate life's upsets and losses. You equally amplify and celebrate the good times and blessings in life. People love being around you at work, at home, and in your community. Continue on your path of fulfillment by adding the practices and strategies in this book for living the 3 Promises. Look for opportunities to help others live their 3 Promises, too.

A SCORE BETWEEN 5 AND 9 INDICATES THAT YOU ARE STRUGGLING TO keep the 3 Promises, or you are having difficulty with one or two promises in particular. You may be doing what you love, but you have little time for joy. You may be helping others, but you're not doing what you love. You may be experiencing joy, but you do not like your job or role in life. The good news is that you are on your way to fulfillment. You already have a foundation of action on which to build. Increase your fulfillment by embracing and implementing the strategies and actions in this book to help you increase your joy, passion, and contribution at home and at work.

A SCORE BETWEEN 0 AND 4 INDICATES THAT YOU ARE NOT ENJOYING LIFE. Your days may be lacking joy. You may be doing a job you dislike, or you may be unemployed. You may feel insignificant, or you may feel that you don't make a difference in the lives of others. Be kind to yourself. You may be down now, but by taking the 3 Promises actions suggested in this book every day (even when you don't feel like it), you can begin changing your life immediately. You'll turn things around. Focus on completing meaningful actions to support each of the 3 Promises every day. You'll see the difference it will make in your life.

It's Your Choice

THE 3 PROMISES ARE LIBERATING BECAUSE THEY SIMPLIFY OUR FOCUS on what's important, yet they leave open what we choose to do to live each promise.

There are many ways to experience joy. There are many paths to a rewarding career. And there are countless ways we can give to others. The freedom of choice is a blessing.

I've dedicated this book to providing you with memorable, unique, and practical strategies to fully live the 3 Promises. Each chapter offers a new tool, a new way of thinking, or a new practice for one or more of the promises.

So let's get going with the First Promise: Find Joy Every Day.

PART 1

Find Joy Every Day

We are shaped by our thoughts; we become what
we think. When the mind is pure, joy follows
like a shadow that never leaves.

—Buddha

CHOICE. THAT'S THE KEY.

Joy comes in many varieties. It's not the same for everyone. The key is to have your own repertoire. You need to have many options for creating joy in your life.

I remember standing in my parents' basement talking to my mother. Mom and Dad had recently retired from a long and successful singing career. They had sung with some of the top entertainers of the day, including Bob Hope, Rich Little, and Joey Bishop. They had sung for thousands of people.

Mom was seated next to a four-drawer filing cabinet. It stored all the sheet music for songs she and Dad had sung over the years. We kept talking and reminiscing as Mom opened the bottom drawer. She reached in and pulled out a folder of sheet music. She opened it up, picked out a song sheet, and started singing the opening verse and chorus of "Tonight" from the Broadway musical, *West Side Story*. Mom smiled and put the sheet music back in the drawer. I said, "That's great."

Mom lit up with a big smile, reached for another drawer, and pulled out a second folder of sheet music. She opened that, too. Smiling brightly, she began singing "When You're Smiling," the song made famous by Louis Armstrong. She closed that drawer and opened the one just above it. Mom reached in again and pulled out another song. She sang that one, too. She must have done the same thing for another twelve songs.

It was awesome to see my mother, sitting there, singing these beautiful songs. I was amazed at how many she could pull out of the cabinet and sing.

1

Your repertoire of joy can be just as impressive. It is within your reach and just as accessible as the sheet music in my mother's four-drawer filing cabinet.

The psychologist Sonja Lyubomirsky captures the essence of the First Promise in her book, *The Myths of Happiness.* She writes, "The scientific evidence delivers three kernels of wisdom—first, that short bursts of gladness, tranquility, or delight are not trivial at all; second, that it's frequency, not intensity, that counts; and third, most of us seem to know this. If you come to understand which individuals, situations, places, things, or even times of day make you feel happy, and then practice increasing the regularity of such moments, you will gain a hedonic tool that will serve you well in times of crisis, when the doctor delivers bad news, and beyond."

There are hundreds of ways to trigger, find, and experience joy in your life. Let's explore some of them now.

The Sticker Story: Positive Triggers

A FEW YEARS AGO I WAS SITTING IN MY OFFICE BY MYSELF, AND I WASN'T feeling good. Yeah, I know. I've made a career of researching, writing, and speaking to groups about how to lead a fulfilling life, but—I admit it—I wasn't having a good day.

So, here's my first question: Where do you look when you're feeling bad? Do your eyes look down, like mine did on that day? In fact, I was looking right down at the floor, at my shoes.

And then I started laughing! There was a little purple dinosaur stuck on my left shoe; a white unicorn and Dora the Explorer were stuck next to each other on the right. I realized that Ariela and Eliana, my little girls, who were two and three years old at the time, had somehow slipped the stickers onto my shoes when I was kissing my wife, Dawn, good-bye that morning. Just thinking about how they'd managed to do this without my noticing made me laugh. But then I laughed even harder when I thought, "It's already 11:15 a.m.! Where had I gone that morning with Barney, Dora, and a white unicorn on my shoes?!"

At that moment I got it. The stickers my little girls had put on my shoes were a positive trigger for me. They instantly made me feel good.

Here's my second question: Where do you look when you're feeling good? Do you look up? That's what I did in my office that morning; I looked up and my day was reset. I couldn't even remember why I was feeling bad.

Experiencing positive emotion gave me a second chance to make the day a good one.

In her research, positive psychology researcher Barbara Fredrickson at the University of North Carolina found that positive emotions widen our attention, increase our intuition, and increase our resilience to adversity.

The late psychology researcher Alice Isen discovered that when we're experiencing positive emotion, we're more kind, more generous, and more helpful.

Richard Davidson, a neuropsychology researcher at the University of Wisconsin, demonstrated that positive emotions help boost our immune systems. And at least three studies have shown that there is a strong connection between living a longer life and experiencing frequent positive emotion.

What's my takeaway from all this? If you lose someone you love, you feel sad. If you're threatened, you feel fear. If you witness an injustice, you feel anger. These are normal and important emotions. But on the whole, positive emotions help you think better and build better relationships with others. People prefer to be around curious and creative people more often than spending time with others who are stuck living in negative emotion.

If you ask the people in your life, I'll bet they'll tell you that when you're experiencing positive emotion you do better work and you're a better leader, spouse, and friend. I know that I'm a better dad to two little girls when I'm experiencing positive emotion.

Think of it this way. When you enter a dark room, what do you do? You reach for the light switch. Because you know when you flip it, just like that, you'll have light.

So, what's your light switch? What turns on your positive emotions?

What positive triggers will help you look up when you're feeling down?

When you trigger positive emotion in yourself, you're more creative. When you trigger positive emotions in others, you bring out their best.

First Promise Actions

What are your positive triggers?

What makes you smile?

What makes you laugh?

What puts you in a creative mood?

What triggers your passion, excitement, and hope?

FOR SOME OF US IT'S LOOKING AT PICTURES OF OUR LOVED ONES. SOME of us listen to a favorite song. Others go for a quick walk or do a little dance. Some read a short, funny story. Others remind themselves of their goals or the things that make them feel grateful.

Take a moment to think about the things that trigger your positive emotions. What you find will help you fulfill the First Promise every day.

The Power of Positive Daily Rituals

I WAS TWELVE YEARS OLD WHEN I WENT TO MY FIRST SUMMER BASKETBALL camp. I was having trouble making free throws and I wanted to learn to shoot the ball like the big kids. There was one player in particular who could always make a free throw, no matter the day, time, or moment in the game.

Observing him closely, I noticed that he did exactly the same thing before each free throw: He put his right foot behind the middle of the free-throw line, bounced the basketball twice, and then lifted it over his head with both hands until the ball touched the back of his neck. He then bounced the ball two more times, paused, looked up at the basket, and took his shot. He made it almost every time.

Today, thirty-six years later, I am impressed with how many rituals athletes follow to help them perform at their best. Yet, many of us do not use the power of daily rituals to bring out our best performance.

Your Rituals

THINK ABOUT YOUR MORNING ROUTINE. WHAT DO YOU DO WHEN YOU WAKE up? Most of us stumble out of bed, take a shower, get dressed, and drink a cup of coffee or tea on our way to work. Our ritual is often hustle and hassle. Some days start out well; others not so well.

Mihaly Csikszentmihalyi, cofounder of positive psychology, wrote in his book *Finding Flow*: "The actual quality of life—what we do, and how we feel about it—will be determined by our thoughts and emotions; by the interpretations we give to chemical, biological, and social processes."

Most of us live our day like we play a slot machine; we pull the lever and then see what happens. That's not a powerful or positive way to live.

Instead Csikszentmihalyi suggests, "The first step in improving the quality of life consists of engineering daily activities so that one gets the most rewarding experiences from them."

Ask what the most successful people you know do at the start of their day. You'll find that most of them follow a ritual that jump-starts their best self. They approach the beginning of their day with the same concentration they would have if they were stepping to the free-throw line.

My Chance

TWO YEARS AFTER BASKETBALL CAMP, I PLAYED IN MY FIRST HIGH SCHOOL freshman basketball game. Our team was down by two points, and I was standing at the free-throw line. There was no time left on the clock. I had a chance to make two free throws to put the game into overtime.

Just as the referee passed me the ball to take my first shot, my mom walked into the gym. She stopped right in my line of sight. Now everyone was looking at me, including my mom. I was nervous. So, I did the little ritual I learned at basketball camp—two bounces, basketball behind my head, two more bounces, pause—and then I shot the ball. I held my breath as the ball arched high and toward the basket. It went in. Time for the second shot. I followed the same ritual exactly. I took my second shot. I held my breath and watched. And the second shot went in. The gym erupted in cheers, and my teammates swarmed around me. And over their shoulders I saw my mom jumping up and down.

Positive rituals can help bring out your best in the big games of your life—but they can also help bring out your best every day. For me, the day begins with at least five minutes of prayer and meditation, five minutes of inspirational reading to stimulate my mind, five minutes of free writing to awaken my creativity, and a few minutes of exercise to stay energized and healthy.

The bottom line is that we have to make time in our daily calendar for powerful rituals—and then we have to do them.

First Promise Actions

THE BEAUTY OF IMPLEMENTING POSITIVE RITUALS IS THE FREEDOM AND THE power they give you to determine how to kick off your day in the best possible way and to create joy before the day starts rolling.

What positive rituals can you invent or adopt in your life?

What are you doing now that brings out your joy?

What can you do to bring out even more joy at the start of your day?

Try at least one of these rituals tomorrow when you wake up, and notice the impact it has on your day.

A Daily Dose of
Awe Meditation
and Gratitude Prayer

HERE'S ONE RITUAL THAT CAN CHANGE YOUR LIFE. FOR MUCH OF THE PAST twenty years, I have begun each day with the same positive ritual: a dose of what I call awe meditation and gratitude prayer.

Experiencing Awe

NO MATTER WHERE I AM, I START THE DAY WITH AWE MEDITATION. AFTER I wake up, I head for the nearest window, open the curtain, and look outside. When I'm at home, I look at the flowers in the garden. When I'm staying at a hotel, I look at the surrounding buildings in all their variety. When I'm in the country, I take in the sheer abundance and beauty of nature. Wherever I am, there is always something interesting to draw my attention. Each time I look out the window, I appreciate that the universe does not revolve around me; it includes me.

Immersed in wonder and awe, the first step in my morning ritual reminds me that the world is much bigger than my life and concerns.

My mother grew up in Maine and often reflects on the beauty of nature. She once said to me, "Think of the beauty of a maple tree. The same force that makes sap run up from its roots to its trunk, against gravity, is the same force that lives within you." She made her point by gently poking me in the stomach and saying, "It's right there inside of you; connect to it." My awe meditation reminds me every morning of the miracles with which I am connected.

Profound Outcomes

THE PSYCHOLOGISTS JONATHAN HAIDT AND DACHER KELTNER WROTE ABOUT awe in Christopher Peterson and Martin Seligman's book, *Character Strengths and Virtues*: "People consistently report that experiences of awe and elevation have profound outcomes, motivating self-improvement, personal change, altruistic intentions and actions, and the devotion to others and the larger community."

In their book, *How God Changes Your Brain*, neurotheologist and medical doctor Andrew Newberg and Mark Robert Waldman, his colleague at the Center for Spirituality and the Mind at the University of Pennsylvania, describe the impact of meditation on the brain: "The neural circuits activated by meditation buffer you from the deleterious effects of aging and stress and give you better control over your emotions. At the very least, such practices help you remain calm, serene, peaceful, and alert. And for nearly everyone, it gives you a positive and optimistic outlook on life."

Gratitude Prayer

THE SECOND STEP OF MY MORNING RITUAL FOCUSES ON GRATITUDE. I give thanks in prayer for everything that I am grateful for. Philosophers and religious teachers have taught us for thousands of years to begin our day by feeling and expressing gratitude for everything and everyone in our lives.

My thanks include being grateful for a new day, a good night's sleep, my health, my family, my close friends, my key supporters in business, and for the important opportunities I have professionally and personally. Wanting to keep their images fresh in my mind, I visualize the people and things I am most grateful to have in my life.

Following my gratitude prayer, I continue to pray for direction, fulfillment, and peace. I reinforce the 3 Promises in my life by including them in my prayers:

Thank you for this most fulfilling day.
I will find joy.
I will do what I love.
I will make a difference.
Thank you for helping me fulfill my 3 Promises today.

Then, I like to say my prayer of fulfillment in the present tense:
I'm finding joy.
I'm doing what I love.
I'm making a difference.
Thank you for this most fulfilling day.

The Benefits of Gratitude and Prayer

ROBERT EMMONS, THE PREEMINENT PSYCHOLOGY RESEARCHER ON gratitude, writes in *Gratitude Works!,* "Clinical trials indicate that the practice [of gratitude] can . . . lower blood pressure, improve immune function, promote happiness and well-being, and spurs acts of helpfulness, generosity, and cooperation."

Newberg and Waldman also include in their research the important benefits associated with prayer. They write, "Activities involving meditation and intensive prayer permanently strengthen neural functioning in specific parts of the brain that are involved with lowering anxiety and depression, enhancing social awareness and empathy, and improving cognitive and intellectual functioning."

First Promise Actions

GIVEN THE POWERFUL HEALTH AND MENTAL BENEFITS OF MEDITATION, consider finding five minutes to meditate every morning. You might try my awe meditation; there is always something around us to appreciate.

If you're inclined to pray, consider including prayer in your morning routine. What prayers do you find inspiring? Add one or two of them to your morning ritual.

The Secret to Getting Back Up

FLOYD PATTERSON, A HEAVYWEIGHT BOXING LEGEND AND HALL OF FAMER, once said, "They said I was the fighter who got knocked down the most, but I also got up the most." Patterson found a way to get back up each time. This is the mark of a good leader, and a successful person. You get up after you get smacked.

All success stories involve knockdown after knockdown. The question is, "Why do some people have the courage and confidence to get up while many people stay down?" Let me tell you how I learned the secret.

Mom

EIGHTEEN YEARS AGO ON A FRIDAY AFTERNOON IN NEW YORK CITY something happened to me at work. I don't remember what, but I know it was one of those events that makes you want to run home, pull the blinds, get under the covers, and put a pillow over your head.

As luck would have it, my mother was visiting me that weekend and was waiting for me when I returned from work. Now, I have a mom with a talent for finding out what's bothering you; I tell everyone she's like a "psychological MRI." All she has to do is give you one hug and one look to know that's something's wrong. She also knows just what to say. This is what she said to me that night.

David, when I was growing up in Maine, our family didn't have a lot of money. When I was very young, we moved to the country. We had an outhouse attached to our home. We had a pump in the kitchen sink. I went to a one-room schoolhouse in the fifth grade. When my sister and I wanted to go to the city school, we picked string beans in the summer to help pay for tuition.

And on cold winter nights after we went to bed, my mother liked to read, so she put her feet up on the oven door to keep warm.

David, we didn't have a lot. And I'm telling you that it wasn't always easy. But my parents taught me something that helped me through life. And I want you to do the same thing.

When you feel overwhelmed and something is getting you down, stop and think of everything you have and everyone you're grateful for.

When you do, it will remind you of the good in your life before you focus on the bad. I promise you'll feel stronger and you'll feel better.

That's how my mother taught me the secret of gratitude.

Sunday night came, and Mom left for home in Milwaukee.

A few hours later, I was walking around the east side of Manhattan. I began to worry about work and was feeling more than just the Sunday night blues. That's when I thought of Mom and what she said, "Think about what you're grateful for."

My Turn

SO I STOPPED RIGHT WHERE I WAS, ABOUT THE MIDDLE OF THE BLOCK ON 20TH Street, between First and Second Avenue, and I backed up against the wall of a white brick elementary school. Looking up, I did just what Mom had told me to do: I thought of everything that I was grateful for. I can still remember the feeling that came next. Almost immediately my heart stopped racing, my chest relaxed, and I took a deep breath. I looked up at the sky and felt as if the passing clouds were carrying my worries away. They no longer seemed important compared to the many things I was grateful for. I felt relief like I'd never felt it before.

From that moment on, I have known the power of gratitude and have tapped into it almost every day over the last eighteen years—some days more than others.

One final note about my mom. That little girl from Maine? She graduated from the New England Conservatory of Music and became a leading singer with the National Opera Company. She performed for Columbia Artists and toured Europe for the U.S. State Department to entertain our troops.

My mother's belief in gratitude gave her the strength and courage to make her life a good one. So the next time you take one on the chin, do as my mom says, "Think of everyone and everything that you are grateful for," and like Floyd Patterson, you'll get back up before the count of ten.

First Promise Actions

INCLUDE GRATITUDE PRAYER OR GRATITUDE MEDITATION IN YOUR RESILIENCE strategy. When something throws you off course, make more room for joy by stopping to acknowledge all the important people in your life. Also plan to use this same strategy to strengthen yourself before you enter an anticipated stressful situation. Make this gratitude practice one of your First Promise activities.

Be a Day-Starter

WHEN I'M NOT ON THE ROAD SPEAKING, I START EACH DAY BY KISSING AND hugging my wife, Dawn. I want her to feel my love before the day gets underway. Then, I quietly walk into my little girls' rooms and give them a big hug and a kiss. I make it my goal to make them laugh, or at least smile, each time I wake them. I sing, play music and dance, make funny faces, piggyback each one out of bed, walk them on my feet, tell stories . . . anything I can do to start their day with joy. It's one of my favorite parts of the day.

When everyone is dressed, we meet in the kitchen and have breakfast together. We talk about what we're most excited about in the day ahead, and joke around at the table. Finally, when it's time for the girls to go to school, we say good-bye with hugs and kisses.

I see it as my mission to help my family start their day in the best possible way. I want them to be in the mood to enjoy everything good that will come to them that day and to be prepared to handle any challenges that might arise. I see my role as a Day-Starter as an opportunity to make a positive difference in the lives of the people I love.

All of us have the same opportunity to decide how to start each day. What is your first interaction of the day? What do you do and say, when you get up in the morning, to help the ones you love?

Your Opportunity

IF YOU'RE NOT ALREADY BEGINNING YOUR DAY AS POSITIVELY AS YOU MIGHT wish, you can change that by expressing your love and friendship with your words and actions.

First Promise Actions

IF YOU NORMALLY COMPLAIN RIGHT AFTER YOU GET UP, EXPRESS YOUR love first. Greet your loved ones with a hug and a kiss. And if you don't normally hug and kiss your family, there's no need to wait. Start making it a First Promise activity.

If you live with roommates, be the first to greet everyone. Be the first to smile. Make the coffee. Offer to make breakfast for everyone when you're making yours. Demonstrate your interest in them. Start their day.

If you live alone, call someone you care about. Email a kind note to a friend. Exercise with a buddy, or grab a cup of coffee with him or her. Start someone's day.

At work, be the first one to smile, say hello, send a nice note, make a supportive call, and offer to help someone in need. Celebrate birthdays, anniversaries, milestones, and accomplishments. Be the one who shares positive, encouraging, and important news. Hold back on excessive complaining, unbalanced criticism, and gossiping.

The most powerful way you can help start the day for people at home or work is to induce their joy. It's a gift you can give every day. Be a Day-Starter.

A Bridge to Your Positive Future

GRATITUDE IS MORE THAN A ROUTINE OR A RESILIENCE STRATEGY. THINK of it as a bridge that spans a river. It must have strong supporting foundations on both banks, without which it would surely collapse. And so it is with the bridge to your positive future. The stronger your foundation of gratitude, the greater the distance your bridge can take you in life. And the strength of your gratitude depends on your awareness of the support you have to achieve your best possible life. The late philosophy professor Robert Solomon said this about gratitude, "One can take one's life and its advantages for granted, but how much better it is to acknowledge not only those advantages but one's gratitude for them."

Gratitude helps you recognize the support that you've received on your path to achieve the life you have. Solomon writes, "It involves an admission of our vulnerability and our dependence on other people."

Gratitude provides you with the courage to pursue your ambition in life. What you remember strengthens your bridge to a positive future. Here are the keys to reinforce your foundation of gratitude and your First Promise:

Key People

GRATITUDE REMINDS YOU OF ALL THE KEY PEOPLE IN YOUR LIFE. THINK OF these individuals now. Who are the people who advise you? Who are the people who challenge you? Who are the people who set you straight when you veer off course? And who are the people who give you a hug when you need one? Be grateful for these people: Strengthen your bridge.

Your Strengths

GRATITUDE REMINDS YOU OF YOUR STRENGTHS, THE KEY TO FULFILLING THE Second Promise: Do What You Love. Think of what comes naturally to you. What do you do well? What do you enjoy doing? What do others say you excel in? What are your gifts? Be grateful for what makes you unique: Strengthen your bridge.

Your Achievements

GRATITUDE REMINDS YOU OF WHAT YOU HAVE ACHIEVED. THINK ABOUT WHAT you've accomplished in your life. What goals have you met? What successes have you enjoyed? Be grateful for your achievements: Strengthen your bridge.

The Wonders Around You

GRATITUDE REMINDS YOU OF THE WONDERS AROUND YOU: THE WARMTH OF the sun, the glow of the moon and stars, the waves of the ocean, the comfort of a breeze, the colors of flowers, the majesty of trees, the speed of planes, the utility of buildings, and the power of trains. Be grateful for the miracles of nature and the wondrous products of man: Strengthen your bridge.

Abundance

DIETRICH BONHOEFFER, THE GERMAN THEOLOGIAN, PASTOR, AND NAZI resister, wrote about gratitude in this way: "In ordinary life we hardly realize that we receive a great deal more than we give, and that it is only with gratitude that life becomes rich."

When you fill your life with gratitude, you will experience the feeling of abundance in your relationships, your strengths, your achievements, and everything that is miraculous and powerful around you. Gratitude strengthens the bridge to your best possible life.

Make the crossing.

First Promise Actions

EXPAND YOUR GRATITUDE PRACTICE TO INCLUDE AN APPRECIATION OF THE key people in your life, your strengths, and your achievements. Reflect periodically on what you do well and what you have accomplished; make it a First Promise activity.

Stop for Gratitude Moments

ONE MORNING, AS I WAS HEADING FROM THE BEDROOM TO THE KITCHEN, I stopped in the foyer to look at two pieces of mail that had been opened and were sitting on a shelf. I had just checked on Dawn and the girls. Dawn was still sleeping, and Eliana and Ariela were sprawled across our bed fast asleep. I reached for the letter on top. It was a letter addressed to Dawn. I read the first two lines: "Thank you for your recent visit to our facility. Your digital mammogram shows no evidence of cancer."

I stopped. I didn't read the rest of the letter. I just thought about what it could have said. And then I thought about all the other letters that were opened that day. I thought about all the women around the world who had received the news they feared the most.

Acknowledgment

THEN, I HAD WHAT I CALL A "GRATITUDE MOMENT."

I looked outside the nearest window and took in the big world. And I said thank you. Thank you for blessing the health of my wife, children, parents, and all of my family. Thank you for caring for my friends and colleagues. And I said thank you for everything that is good in my life.

I know letters and phone calls could come at any time with news I would never want to hear. So, when I am reminded of the good in my life, I stop and say thank you. I want to always appreciate the abundance in my life.

The evidence is overwhelming: Gratitude pays dividends to all who practice it. Embrace gratitude moments when they happen and you will fulfill your First Promise.

First Promise Actions

WHENEVER YOU EXPERIENCE A GRATITUDE MOMENT, ACT ON IT AND GIVE thanks. Then write about what happened and why you were inspired. It will serve as a record of the good things in your life.

Act on Gratitude Impulses

THE PRE-KINDERGARTEN GRADUATION CEREMONY FOR MY YOUNGER daughter, Ariela, was adorable. She and all the kids were wonderful. Ariela's cap was made of white felt with a gold tassel, and her gown was one of my white dress shirts that she wore backwards. We took pictures, clapped, laughed, and yelled, "Ariela! Yay, Ariela!" She waved back and smiled. It was a beautiful morning.

Later that night, after Dawn and the girls went to sleep, I started working again. I'd been back at my desk writing for about an hour when it hit me. I became overwhelmed with gratitude. I stopped what I was doing. I leaned back, and I closed my eyes. I knew that my daughter's graduation—my daughter's life—would not be possible without my wife, Dawn. She gave birth to our daughters and cares for them every day. She is a wonderful mother.

Opportunity

DOES THIS EVER HAPPEN TO YOU? YOU ARE IN THE MIDDLE OF DOING something when all of a sudden you feel thankful for someone important in your life? You may be working, reading, exercising, meditating, or praying. And without warning, you become overwhelmed by a feeling of gratitude.

I call these moments of clarity "gratitude impulses." These experiences remind us of what matters to us in our lives.

But like all emotions, gratitude impulses can be fleeting. We feel the initial emotion. We pause. We reflect.

But then we get back to what we were doing. We just keep on going.

I ask you to try another way. Act on your gratitude impulses. Don't let the opportunity pass by: It is one of the easiest ways for you to fulfill the First Promise (and the Third Promise, too).

Gratitude impulses are authentic expressions of who we are and what's important to us. They reflect our unguarded selves. They remind us of the important people in our lives. They call our attention to what we care about.

In these moments, we don't feel self-conscious. We don't evaluate our feelings. We just feel grateful. This is the time for us to act.

Do It

WHEN WE FEEL GRATEFUL TO PEOPLE, WE SHOULD LET THEM KNOW. AND we can make it quick: We just need to let them know how we feel. We should express our gratitude before we start rationalizing why now is not the time. Sure, we can think about the best way to express our appreciation, but we should not let our thoughtful deliberation lead to inaction.

We can do the same thing in the workplace and act on our gratitude impulses. When we genuinely feel grateful to others at work, we should express it. Let people know. Tell them why. Be specific. Research tells us that we all value being told how much we matter.

One day we may not be able to reach the people we love and care about. Why let our gratitude impulses go unexpressed? Embrace feelings of gratitude each time they come.

So I grabbed a pen and a card for Dawn. I wrote how much I appreciated everything she does for the girls, and how much I love her. I sealed the card in an envelope, and I left it in front of the coffee maker for her to read first thing in the morning.

First Promise Actions

MAKE THANKING SOMEONE AT HOME OR AT WORK ONE OF YOUR FIRST Promise activities. Amplify the impact of the gratitude you feel for people by acknowledging them right away. Again, write down what happened and how you expressed your gratitude.

The Gratitude Path

ON MY WAY TO CHICAGO TO LEAD A CORPORATE SEMINAR, A COUPLE YEARS ago, I found myself walking down the aisle of a very full plane. My seat was 22C. To my surprise, there was no one beside me, and no one behind me. I felt like I had won the lottery of airplane seating. You know the feeling—you can spread out, recline without bothering anyone, and even use two tray tables.

I needed to concentrate on reviewing my presentation notes. The peace and quiet would be great. I immediately opened my bag and began to work. The flight attendants were readying the plane for takeoff when it happened.

"You're in 23C," I heard a flight attendant say. And just as I looked up, I heard the increasingly loud cries of a baby. A mother and her upset baby girl were coming my way. Seat 23C was right behind me.

The baby cried even harder when her mom took her seat.

Five minutes later the baby's cries turned into a steady wail, and her little legs began kicking my seat. And the kicks kept coming: hard, soft, three in repetition, followed by stiff legs pushing on the back of the chair, and then the jackhammer. There was no way that I could continue to work.

I had a lot of questions, but I had no answers. "Why does the little girl have to kick my seat? Isn't there a way to stop her from crying? And why of all places on the plane does she have to sit right behind me!?" I started searching for what I could say, or what I should do, but there was nowhere to go.

A Fork in the Path

THEN I SMILED. I REALIZED I ACTUALLY HAD A CHOICE. I COULD EITHER SEE the situation as a dead-end negative, or I could see the situation in another way. I could find another road out and take it. And I did. In that moment I found another way to look at the situation: I now call it a "gratitude path."

I thought of my own children and started to laugh when I remembered that Eliana and Ariela had done their share of crying and seat kicking in airplanes, as hard as Dawn and I had tried to stop them. So, I turned the baby's crying and seat kicking into a reminder that I have two wonderful little girls of my own. Each time the little girl cried or kicked my seat, I felt grateful for my daughters. I smiled and even laughed.

Sure, I would have preferred the flight to be quieter. But guess what? I was able to work because I became quieter inside. I replaced the negative emotion I was feeling with gratitude for my own children. The psychologist Barbara Frederickson observed how inducing positive emotions in people following a negative experience loosens the vice grip that the negative event holds psychologically.

When we landed in Chicago, I stood up and turned to look at the mother and her child. She smiled nervously and started to apologize for her daughter's crying. I stopped her. I pulled out my wallet, opened it, and handed a picture to her. I pointed to my two little red-headed daughters and said, "These are my little girls. They're wonderful. And they cried a lot, too. Your daughter is beautiful. Congratulations."

She smiled and said, "Thank you."

I smiled and left the plane feeling good (something I wouldn't have thought possible when the crying and kicking began).

The point is that we can fixate on the things that annoy us and raise the level of needless negative emotion, or we can quickly pivot to something that triggers positive emotion and let joy back into our day.

First Promise Actions

THE NEXT TIME A SITUATION SEEMS TO BE A FRUSTRATING DEAD-END OF negativity, ask yourself, "What's my gratitude path?" There's almost always another route you can take. Make sure to record your positive response in your writing.

The Power of Your Gratitude Chain

EVERYTHING GOOD THAT HAPPENS IN THIS WORLD IS THE RESULT OF A CHAIN of events. No matter the size, each event in our life has a history of activity. Unfortunately, most of us are unaware of the many good links in each chain of events.

Consider the last time you opened a can of beans. Think about who planted, picked, packed, shipped, stocked, and then sold them to you. Most of us wouldn't think about that. We would just open the can, put the beans on our plate, pop them in the microwave, grab a fork, and start eating them as soon as the plate is put on the table. We wouldn't see the chain, we would just see the beans.

My mom knows about beans, and she understands the chain because she picked beans while growing up in Maine. During the summer, Mom and her sister would walk down the hill from their home to the Kennebec River, pay ten cents for someone to ferry them to the other side in a rowboat, and then head for the bus that would take them to the farm where the beans were grown. Mom would spend all day in the hot sun picking string beans, earning ten dollars a week. Then the beans were sorted, washed, packed, and trucked to nearby grocery stores.

So when Mom sits down to eat string beans, she appreciates the chain. Her awareness of all the people and effort that it takes to get beans from the farm to her plate makes her feel grateful. And that's a good thing.

Robert Emmons wrote in his book, *Thanks! How the New Science of Gratitude Can Make You Happier,* "Grateful people experience higher levels of positive emotions such as joy, enthusiasm, love, happiness, and optimism, and that the practice of gratitude as a discipline protects a person from the destructive impulses of envy, resentment, greed, and bitterness."

Gratitude Chains

THE CHALLENGE THEN IS FOR US TO FIND WAYS OF BECOMING MORE grateful. One powerful way to increase your gratitude is by increasing the number of what I call "Gratitude Chains" in your life. Gratitude Chains are made up of links of appreciation for the people and things we care about. These are the four keys to building Gratitude Chains:

Cultivate Awareness
EVERY DAY, LOOK AROUND AND TAKE NOTE OF WHAT YOU VALUE. WHAT AND who do you appreciate in your life? (For example, your spouse, your children, your job, your daily meals, your friends, your country, your car, your home, the customer service you receive, the coffee you drink, and so on). Write down what you observe. Make this a part of your First Promise fulfillment.

Cultivate Curiosity
LEARN MORE ABOUT EACH PERSON OR ITEM ON YOUR LIST. HOW DO THESE people do what they do each day? What contributes to these important things in your life? Ask questions, study, and research. Do whatever you have to do in order to better understand what and whom you treasure.

Cultivate Memory
YOU ONLY FEEL GRATEFUL FOR WHAT YOU REMEMBER. PRACTICE RECALLING the most important people and the things you care about in your life. Recite them in the morning. Add them to your prayers. Journal about them. Reflect on them each day. Thank them.

Create Gratitude Chains

THERE IS POWER IN THE GRATITUDE CHAIN. THE MORE WE KNOW ABOUT THE people and the things that matter to us in our lives, the more likely we will feel grateful. The gratitude you feel will infuse energy into your 3 Promises activities.

Building a Personal Gratitude Chain

LET'S LOOK AT HOW A GRATITUDE CHAIN CAN BE APPLIED TO YOUR PERSONAL life: You can start with your spouse, boyfriend or girlfriend, or a friend. If you do not fully appreciate what they do and how they do it every day, step into their world. Here's an example of a Gratitude Chain I created around my wife, Dawn.

Step One: Cultivate Awareness

FOR A NUMBER OF YEARS WHEN MY DAUGHTERS WERE YOUNGER, DAWN drove our daughters, Eliana and Ariela, forty-five minutes each way to school, Monday through Friday. She often had to make two round trips because the girls got out of school at different times. My girls received the education we wanted for them because Dawn made the drive every day. I did not truly experience gratitude for what she did until I made the trip a number of times myself. I became aware.

I also did not fully understand the demands of a mother's role until I spent entire days—morning until bedtime—with the girls. My gratitude increased when I realized how much love, patience, and stamina Dawn draws on every day. In fact, I have an appreciation for all moms. I became aware.

Step Two: Cultivate Curiosity

I ASKED DAWN HOW SHE MANAGED EVERY MORNING TO BATHE, DRESS, FEED, brush hair, put on sunscreen, make lunches, fill backpacks, and put on shoes for the girls so quickly. I wanted to know her secret (because, truthfully, it takes me twice as long to do the same thing). I asked about her system for accomplishing what she seems to do so effortlessly. I learned the steps to each task, but more importantly, I learned how much love, care, and thought Dawn put into each day with the girls. I became curious.

Step Three: Cultivate Memory

EVERY MORNING WHEN I WAKE UP, I START THE DAY BY RECITING EVERYTHING
I am grateful for, and Dawn is at the top of my list. This gratitude ritual
helps me remember anew all that she does for our family each day.

Then I look for opportunities, big and small, to recognize Dawn. One
practice is to write her notes that congratulate or thank her. And they
always say that I love her. I commit my gratitude to memory by practicing
gratitude. I remember.

Gratitude Chains help to embed in our subconscious positive thoughts
and feelings about who and what we care about; they keep our minds
focused on recognizing everyone and everything that is important to us.
And the more Gratitude Chains we build, the more the opportunities we'll
have to influence our own happiness.

Building a Business Gratitude Chain

CREATING A GRATITUDE CHAIN IS ALSO AN EFFECTIVE LEADERSHIP TOOL
in business.

I interviewed Arthur J. Kobacker before he passed away at the age of
83. Art was a business leader and philanthropist. One endeavor that was
most rewarding to him personally involved providing leadership and the
initial funding (and supplemental annual funds) needed to build and support
Village Academy, a K–12 school in the heart of Delray Beach, Florida's inner
city. (His wife, Sara Jo, daughter, Peggy Shiffrin, and son, Alfred continue
that support today.) Art was also a successful businessman. In 1994, he sold
The Kobacker Company's 679 stores (located in thirty-one states) to Payless
ShoeSource Inc.

In our two-hour interview, Art shared some of his experiences in
business and in life. He believed in the importance of building Gratitude
Chains in business, and believed that successful business leaders should
always connect directly with their customers and their employees.

So let's look at a Gratitude Chain focused on business and include Art's
insights to illustrate each part of the Gratitude Chain–building process.

Step One: Cultivate Awareness

SPEND TIME IN YOUR STORES. VISIT YOUR CUSTOMER SERVICE CENTERS.

Art told me about a time when an international group of businessmen came to visit him for a week, but they arrived one week early. Art was out of town visiting a store, so someone from his office called his wife, Sara Jo, to ask if she knew where he was.

Art said, "I remember my wife started making some calls . . . and she reached the store in Portsmouth, Virginia, talked to a very nice store manager, and she said, 'Is Mr. Kobacker there?' And he said, 'No, he's not.' 'And had he been there?' 'No.' 'Is he expected?' And this manager said, 'He is always expected.'"

Step Two: Cultivate Curiosity

ASK YOUR CUSTOMERS WHAT THEY VALUE AND LIKE BEST ABOUT YOUR products and services. Ask them what they would like you to improve.

Talk to your employees. Ask them what helps them support your customers the most—and in the best way—and what makes it hard for them to do their job.

Art told me, "If you ask the right questions, you get the right answers, and you find out where you are making mistakes and where you are doing things that are right—and then you expand on that. I just learned a whole lot from doing that. Visiting stores, meeting with people, the store employees and the store manager, and talking to customers, were the high points of my retail experience."

Step Three: Cultivate Memory

RECOGNIZE PUBLICLY AND PRIVATELY THE EMPLOYEES WHO BEST SERVICE your customers. Include "great service" stories in your talks and interviews; spread the word that customer service is prized in your company, and pay personal visits to your best employees.

"We had a particular store manager by the name of Bob Mallick," Art remembered.

"He was in Belle Vernon, Pennsylvania, in a Picway Shoe Store, and I used to say at various times, 'Let's fly to Belle Vernon and worship at the feet of Bob Mallick.' So here we would come flying in on a plane with the head of our store operations, our regional vice president, the district supervisor for that area, the men's buyer, the women's shoe buyer, and the children's shoe buyer, and so on. And we would all arrive in the store, and we would ask Bob Mallick, 'What do you need?'"

Art concluded, "I always felt that I could learn so much from a store manager who had to deal with the customer every day, all day long."

The best leaders build Gratitude Chains in their business. They make it clear who and what they value. Arthur J. Kobacker knew how to build Gratitude Chains in business. And the beauty of Art was that he knew how to build Gratitude Chains at home and in the community, too.

First Promise Actions

WHAT IF YOU CREATED A GRATITUDE CHAIN FOR ALL THE IMPORTANT PEOPLE at home and at work? You would substantially increase your gratitude for these people. Fulfill your First Promise by scheduling and building a gratitude chain each month or at any time you want to better understand and appreciate someone.

Make What You're Wearing Meaningful

WHEN I WAS GROWING UP, WE WOULD PUT A RUBBER BAND ON OUR WRIST IF we wanted to remember something. The rubber band represented an action we were supposed to take later in the day. Once we did what we had intended to do, we took off the band. And we would repeat the ritual any time we needed help remembering something. A few years ago this idea was carried to another level.

Millions of people across the country began wearing even thicker rubber bands on their wrists. These bands came imprinted with an inspirational message. Many people have worn these bands for years, never removing them from their wrists.

This phenomenon fascinated me. So, I conducted an informal survey with people who were wearing these bands. I asked each one, "When you look at your band each day, how does it help you?" With few exceptions each person I polled said something like, "You know, I mostly forget I'm wearing it." Most of them would then tell me the original inspiration for putting it on their wrist. The challenge was that they were seldom consciously aware of the message they were wearing in the weeks, months, and years that followed.

Wedding rings are another example. How many times over the years have we stopped, looked at our ring, and repeated the vows that we made to our spouse on our wedding day?

A ritual object, whether it's a band or a ring, loses its power to positively influence our lives if it does not remind us of its intended significance.

For thousands of years, the great religions have tried to counteract the tendency of their followers to forget what's most important in life. Religions prescribe rituals that combine self-reflection, physical action, and the use of objects to inspire their followers to lead a virtuous life.

So if you choose to wear or carry something, whether it's a band, a ring, a charm, a picture, or anything else, make sure that the message it represents is personally meaningful and memorable.

If these ritual acts were worth doing once; their meaning is worth remembering always.

First Promise Actions

LET YOUR RITUAL OBJECTS REMIND YOU TO BE YOUR BEST SELF EVERY DAY. Let them remind you of everything for which you are grateful. Let them remind you of the best life you can imagine living. Let them remind you of the 3 Promises: Find Joy Every Day, Do What You Love, and Make a Difference. Make a review of your ritual objects a part of your First Promise activities.

Talking to Yourself
Can Make You Happier

ONCE, WHEN WE WERE WALKING THROUGH A NATURE PRESERVE, MY daughter Eliana, who was four years old at the time, stopped, turned around, looked right up at me, and said, "Papi, what did you say?"

I said, "Ah, nothing sweetie."

"But Papi, I heard you say something."

"Oh, Eliana, I must have been talking to myself."

And then she asked me the question, "Papi, why were you talking to yourself?"

Why was I talking to myself? That was a great question. I didn't even know that I was doing it.

While you might be smiling right now, you know you do it, too. We all do it. If you don't believe me, try this quick exercise.

Take a quick break, and send me an email about what you've read so far in this chapter. You can reach me at david@davidjpollay.com. Okay?

Stop. Now what did you say to yourself? In all likelihood you said something along the lines of: "Why is he asking me to do this?" "I don't have time right now." "I don't do exercises." "I'm not emailing an author." That's all self-talk—something that all of us do. And that's okay, as it turns out.

Research says we can speak approximately 200 words per minute out loud, yet we speak on average more than 1,300 words to ourselves per minute. At this rate we might have over 45,000 thoughts per day. The problem is that many of these thoughts aren't helpful.

What does all of this mean for us? The psychologist Roy Baumeister has found in his research that people remember bad events more often than good events. So, if we are more likely to remember the bad stuff, and we talk to ourselves at an incredible speed, how much of what we say to ourselves helps us live a better life? Are we more successful, and are we happier?

A Lesson

TWENTY-FOUR YEARS AGO MY GRANDFATHER TAUGHT ME THAT THE answer to that question can be "yes," if we choose what to say to ourselves. He taught me the power of self-talk.

I was visiting my eighty-six-year-old grandfather—we called him Bumpa Trask—at his home in Augusta, Maine. Bumpa was having a rough morning; he was not feeling well. The survivor of three major strokes, Bumpa had a right to feel bad. Sometimes he would feel the lingering effects.

That morning, I walked down the short hallway from the guest bedroom to the kitchen. I stopped when I heard his voice. I slowly peeked around the corner and saw him sitting in his rocking chair. He was staring at his legs as he said, "Legs don't fail me now. You can do it. You've always been strong. I have a lot to do. Let's go legs. I'm getting up."

Thirty minutes later Bumpa was outside in the backyard chopping wood. Here was a man the doctors thought we could have lost three times. He lived to be ninety years old.

We are at our best when we think about all the support we have, the strengths we have been given, the successes we've had, and the goals we have now. We're at our best when we choose what to think about.

And it was my four-year-old daughter's question that reminded me to choose the self-talk that helps me live a fulfilling life. Consider which mantras, prayers, and other things you can say to yourself that will help you fulfill the 3 Promises every day.

One More Story

TWO YEARS AGO I WAS IN A BIBLE STUDY MEETING, SEATED IN THE FRONT row, when along comes a woman, slowly walking across the front of the room, pulling an oxygen tank on wheels. She sits down and breathes with obvious effort.

The meeting starts, and she actively participates. She makes jokes, offers insights, and interacts with others.

After the meeting, I walk over to her and introduce myself. She tells me her name is Sybil. And after a few questions, she tells me that she is eighty-nine.

"Wow!" I say. "I'm so impressed with your spirit. You have such a contagious positive attitude. Do you do anything in particular each day to help you be so positive?"

She said, "After I wake up and pass in front of the mirror for the first time, I stop, look at myself, and say, 'Nice to see you.' It reminds me that I'm alive, and it reminds me to appreciate myself. I want to live my life fully."

Postscript

I WAS PLANNING ON GIVING A SIGNED COPY OF THE 3 PROMISES TO SYBIL. She was so pleased when I told her that I had included her story. Unfortunately, Sybil passed away before I could finish the book. Her life and her passing remind me how important it is to make everyday a fulfilling one. We do not know which day will be our last, or the last day for the people we love. Being able to say "nice to see you" to ourselves and to the people we care about is a blessing to be appreciated *every day*.

First Promise Actions

INCREASE YOUR JOY BY INCREASING YOUR POSITIVE AND CONSTRUCTIVE self-talk. When you catch yourself in the midst of limiting and destructive self-talk, redirect your internal conversation to something expanding and constructive. Recognize your accomplishment, and write it down.

The Rule of the Narrator

THERE'S NO GETTING AWAY FROM SELF-TALK. THERE'S ALWAYS CHATTER going on in our head. No matter what we're doing, there is always an inner voice saying something.

Over the years, I have learned a critical secret to success. I call it "The Rule of the Narrator." The voice that narrates our life helps determine our success, and it makes joy possible in our lives.

The Introduction

THERE WAS A HUM OF CONVERSATION AS THE AUDIENCE SETTLED IN. THE band members quietly took their places on a dimly lit stage. The theater operator brought the lights down. The audience grew quiet in anticipation. The emcee entered stage left, the spotlight following him. The audience welcomed him with applause.

The drummer started a quiet drum roll. Speaking in a deep voice, the emcee told us about the act we were about to see. He mesmerized the audience with a story of accomplishment and adventure. The drummer and emcee engaged in a choreographed dance of excitement: The drum roll accentuated the words as he spoke them, providing them with more energy and creating the power of anticipation that a great event was about to take place. And all at once, the emcee called out their names, the band started playing, the act entered stage right, the spotlight swung over to meet them, the audience erupted in applause, and the singers launched into their first song in full voice.

I saw this introduction many times. And each time my parents would come on stage, standing tall, walking confidently, chest out, arms extended, and smiling with the majesty of a king and queen. The stage was their castle and the theater their kingdom. The audience believed they were in for a magnificent journey. And so did my parents. They were ready to sing.

It was during these years when I was growing up that I learned the power of words and music in setting the stage for greatness. When my parents listened to the emcee introduce them, they focused on their mission. The words and music they heard centered their attention. They believed in themselves, and they were committed to giving their best performance.

All great performers, athletes, and leaders are introduced in a similarly captivating way. The audience and the performer are made to share a powerful narrative that what they are about to experience is going to be spectacular.

It's Your Choice . . . and Your Voice

YOUR LIFE IS NOT A SILENT MOVIE. IN FACT, IT IS ONE THAT YOU NARRATE every moment of the day. Sometimes your narrator is an emcee, a host, or an announcer. But, most of the time the voice is yours. You are introducing your every activity and narrating your every move consciously and unconsciously.

Just think for a moment about today. What have you been narrating? As my daughter reminded me, we're talking to ourselves all the time.

What words have you been using? If you have been repeating, "I'm tired," "I don't feel like doing that," or "I'm worried," you are limiting your ability to perform at your best. But if you say instead, "I'm excited," "I'm ready," and "I can," you engage some of your best energy to support yourself. The bottom line is that "The Rule of the Narrator" is always in play, and you are the narrator.

Throughout each day you have an opportunity to choose your narrator. And you determine what is said and how it is said. When you wake up, see your loved ones, face a challenge, start a project, encounter a problem, join a meeting, work on a task, and see an opportunity, you have a chance to narrate your story in a powerful way. You get to choose the words and soundtrack of your life. Your mind sets the stage for your performance.

So the next time you begin to fulfill one of your 3 Promises, bring out your best narrator. Cue the band, turn on the spotlight, listen to the emcee's introduction, hear the audience applaud, and enter in full voice. It's your stage. Bring the house down.

First Promise Actions

PAY PARTICULAR ATTENTION TO YOUR NARRATION IMMEDIATELY PRIOR TO important activities. Make it a First Promise activity to recognize yourself when your narration is empowering. And acknowledge yourself when you change a negative narration to a positive one. Keep track of your successes, and write them down.

Don't Play Email Lottery

AFTER I WAVED GOODBYE TO DAWN AND THE GIRLS AS THEY LEFT THE HOUSE one morning, I went back into the house, grabbed a cup of tea, and sat down at the computer. I went straight to my four email accounts and started reading all the email and social media messages that had arrived overnight. Thirty minutes later, I had responded to just a third of them: I had to stop to drive to my office in time for a meeting. But as I made my way downtown, I was still thinking about the emails I had read but not answered. I was not focusing my energy and creativity on my goals for the day.

How many of you do this every day? How many of you sit down at your computer and say, "Let's see what I have waiting for me today?" You catch yourself hoping that the messages are not delivering bad news or problems for you or that great news is going to appear. Most of us follow this routine from time to time, and many of us do it every day.

Other People's Priorities

BUT HERE'S WHAT'S REALLY HAPPENING: TAKE EMAIL FOR EXAMPLE. WHEN you download your email, you're attending to other people's priorities first. You're going into your day without a plan—without committing to an agenda. In effect, you're bowing to the concerns of others, regardless of their relative importance.

Messages always come with an attachment: the senders' mood. They transmit their worries, anxieties, frustrations, anger, and impatience.

Thankfully, some senders also communicate joy, gratitude, optimism, and excitement.

Now, there's nothing wrong with email and social media: They are vital for communication. They allow us to connect with people all over the world inexpensively and almost instantly. But hoping that good news will appear each time you log on is like playing the lottery: You secretly hope the number of the winning ticket is waiting for you.

The challenge is that if you have not outlined what you must accomplish during the day to advance your goals and dreams, you will get caught up in everyone else's priorities. You will push "your goals" off while you handle the requests of others. Following this strategy, you will never build the momentum you need to live your best possible life.

It's not just about you. When you fail to make progress in the key areas of your life, you feel frustrated and disappointed. And when you feel this way, you create a wave of negative energy that touches many people: Your family, your friends, your colleagues, and your customers will be affected by your negative emotions.

First Promise Actions

MAKE YOUR 3 PROMISES INSTEAD: BEGIN WITH A PLAN BEFORE YOU OPEN your email and social media accounts. Grab your morning beverage and review your goals. And then ask these questions:

What can I do to bring joy to my day?

What can I do today that will bring out my best and express what I love to do?

What can I do to help others today?

Then, with your plan in hand, it's safe to log on. You can determine if anything has arrived that demands your immediate attention. If it does, slide it into place. If it doesn't, respond later.

Respect your own priorities. Believe your goals are worth pursuing. Remember that there are people counting on you to succeed.

Set your own agenda, and Find Joy Every Day.

Look for Beauty and Opportunity

ONE MORNING MY YOUNGER DAUGHTER, ARIELA, AND I WENT TO A LITTLE café for breakfast. After our meal, I held her hand, and we went for a walk in an old residential neighborhood.

About five minutes into our walk, Ariela said, "Papi, look at that tree."

I looked up and saw a fairly common-looking tree without many leaves.

"Not there Papi," Ariela said as she pointed. "Look up there!"

I looked up higher. And at the top of the tree was a burst of orange color. I had never seen anything like it before. It was absolutely beautiful. It looked like a giant bouquet of orange flowers perched on the tree's canopy.

With Ariela's attention and enthusiasm, I saw beauty I had not seen before.

We know from my book *The Law of the Garbage Truck* that it's all too easy to notice the things that frustrate and distract us. People remind us all the time through their complaints, criticisms, gossip, and rumors. But we know it doesn't have to be this way.

Explore

YOU CAN MAKE IT A POINT TO BE AN EXPLORER OF BEAUTY. YOU CAN NOTICE what makes your loved ones special and tell them so. What do you appreciate about your spouse that you've not thought about lately, or possibly have never acknowledged? Let her know, and make her feel great. What about your home is just right for you? Remind yourself of what is special about where you live, your neighborhood, and how happy your children are.

In your meetings, telephone conversations, and impromptu chats, you can look for just one thing of beauty, novelty, or curiosity. Be on the lookout for things you may not have seen or considered before. Listen to new ideas. Ask for input. Welcome feedback. Be the one to look for opportunity in your interactions. When you do that, you'll have fulfilled the First Promise.

Look for a "burst of orange color" in all areas of your life.

First Promise Actions

BE ON THE LOOKOUT FOR BEAUTY WHEREVER YOU ARE. MAKE NOTES IN YOUR journal, or make notes on your phone. Take pictures. Talk to your family and colleagues. Ask questions.

Focus your attention. Turn off the television, radio, cell phone, and computer more often than you normally do. Drive without the radio on, and roll down your windows if possible. Wake up earlier. Go outside. Take another route to work. Invite someone interesting to lunch.

Make a conscious effort to take a break from your routine: This is when you will notice things that you typically miss because you are moving too quickly to observe them.

Include these activities in your First Promise repertoire of joy activities.

Are You Laughing?

DICK ROBINSON, A PULITZER PRIZE–NOMINATED JOURNALIST AND FORMER medical writer for *The Oakland Press*, told me a few years ago that his day doesn't start until his wife, Brenda, makes him laugh. Dick credits his wife for helping to make his life enjoyable. The Robinsons have been married for forty-six years.

In *The Relationship Cure*, psychologist John Gottman writes, "Turning toward one another's sense of humor in everyday situations bolsters your relationships while making life together a lot more fun." It also helps couples stay together. Gottman found in his research that a lack of laughter was often the reason couples divorced later in life. Humor is good for marriages. My father gives it away every time. My mom says, "You can see your father's thinking about something funny when his lips start to quiver and his eyes light up. And when you catch him with that expression, he just starts laughing. He's always looking for the joy in life." After fifty years of marriage, Mom and Dad laugh as often as ever. Their good humor has helped them face the challenges that come with aging.

Good for Us

THE DIRECTOR OF THE FAMED HARVARD STUDY OF ADULT DEVELOPMENT and author of *Aging Well*, George Vaillant, found that the key to successful aging is the ability to cope with life's difficulties. In particular, he found that employing mature defenses like the use of humor is a potent coping strategy. Vaillant writes, "Humor allows us to look directly at what is painful. Humor permits the expression of emotion without individual discomfort and without unpleasant effects upon others." Humor is good for aging.

Heidi Goff, a division general manager when I was a director at MasterCard in the mid 1990s, has the ability to get the most out of a business meeting. Heidi does all that you might expect from a successful senior executive—she's clear on the focus of her meetings, she communicates what's expected of everyone, and she listens carefully and speaks with purpose. Heidi also has the unique ability to inject humor into any situation so that people stay relaxed, creative, and open-minded. She knows when a good laugh or a lighthearted comment will release tension in the room.

"In my own research with executives," says the psychologist Dachter Keltner in his book, *Born to Be Good,* "laughter early in negotiations—the product of break-the-ice banter about families, travel mishaps, hotel rooms, golf games, and the like—sets the stage for mutually beneficial bargaining." Humor is good for business.

The psychologist Willibald Ruch is one of the world's leading researchers on humor. He has found in his research that "habitual laughter can affect physiological changes for the better in musculoskeletal, cardiovascular, endocrine, immunological, and/or neural systems."

We value people in our lives who consistently know how to cheer us up and increase our enjoyment in life. Anytime you can answer "yes" to the question, "Are you laughing?" it's a good thing. Take the opportunity to experience the lighter side of life!

First Promise Actions

THINK ABOUT ALL THE WAYS YOU CAN BRING HUMOR INTO YOUR LIFE. WATCH a comedy show, listen to a podcast, skip in public, tell a joke. Do anything to help you enjoy your day. Plan these First Promise activities, and record their impact on you.

PART 2

Do What You Love

*"Success is not the key to happiness.
Happiness is the key to success.
If you love what you are doing,
you will be successful."*

—Albert Schweitzer

APPROXIMATION. BEST GUESS. THAT'S ALL YOU NEED TO GET STARTED. You don't have to know exactly where you're going—you just need to start by taking a step today. Then, you can start again tomorrow and take another step.

The path to discovering what you love to do is illuminated by your actions. Your passion lights it up as you go. Nothing tricky is involved: Just observe what makes you excited, exhilarated, energetic, confident, and at peace. That's all you need to do. Goals, plans, and visions will come. They just don't have to come today. You'll get there. But today your best guess will do, because anything that expresses what you love to do is rewarding in itself. Your daily promise to do what you love is an acknowledgment that you have something special to share with the world: your family, friends, business, and community.

This part of the book will give you strategies to help uncover what you're most passionate about and what is truly beautiful and unique about your talents. Your vision will become clearer. You'll better appreciate the opportunities you have now, you'll better understand what you want to do, and you'll know how to do more of it every day. The momentum will build because you will be actively fulfilling your Second Promise with daily actions that support your goals.

You're going to design a life that embraces what you love to do. You will integrate your passion and all your talents more fully into your career. What once felt separate—career and passion—will now be one.

A Dream Can Change Your Life

IN 1986, WHEN I WAS A JUNIOR IN COLLEGE, I HAD A DREAM THAT CHANGED my life.

In the dream, I was trapped inside a large office building. I couldn't find a way out. I looked everywhere, ran down hallways, and cut through offices, but there were no exits.

At last, I saw a staircase in the distance and ran toward it. As I approached, I realized that the stairs were behind a wall. I dropped my shoulder and broke through it. I landed on the steps and started to climb as fast as I could, but there were no exits.

I began to panic. What if there was no escape? And then, far above me, I saw a thin line of light under a door that appeared to be an exit. I sprinted toward it and lunged for the door, which flew open. I kept running, but to my horror, I realized that I was on the steep roof of a very tall skyscraper, and I was quickly sliding down. I tried to stop, but my momentum was too great. As I careened toward the edge of the roof, I knew my life would soon be over. At the last moment, my right hand caught a lip on the edge of the roof, and I held on to it with everything I had. I was now dangling by my fingertips, a hundred stories above the ground.

Meaning

AND THEN I WOKE UP. ALTHOUGH I WAS SOAKED WITH SWEAT, BREATHING heavily, and my heart was racing, my mind was completely clear. The symbolism of the dream was evident: My future was literally clinging to a decision I had to make, one I had been thinking about for months. I needed to find out what I really wanted to do with my life and could no longer stand to let life's opportunities pass me by.

And so I made the decision to pursue my interests. I took one year off from school and worked part time to cover the expense of my exploration. I went to concerts, lectures, plays, museums, and I became a deejay at the campus radio station. I joined AIESEC, an international leadership organization located on more than 2,400 university campuses in more than 124 countries and territories. Through AIESEC I represented the United States at an international congress in Innsbruck, traveled throughout Western and Eastern Europe, and worked in West Berlin for two months. And then I received a scholarship from the Yale Center for British Art to study in London for the summer.

Your Dream

THE POINT IS THAT I DID NOT PLAN ANY OF THESE OPPORTUNITIES; THEY were the result of exploration, a search that led me to a whole new set of possibilities and a better understanding of what I love and do well.

Do you want to do more of what you love? What if you could make time to do it? There is a way, and you don't have to drop out of school or leave your job to do it. Now is the time to craft your life to include your passions and to call upon your strengths.

The thirteenth-century poet and mystic, Rumi, wrote, "Though we seem to be sleeping, there is an inner wakefulness that directs the dream, and that will eventually startle us back to the truth of who we are."

What are your dreams telling you?

Second Promise Actions

PAY CLOSE ATTENTION TO YOUR DAYDREAMS AND TO YOUR DREAMS AT night. Listen for what's really important to you. Make it a Second Promise activity to write down any of your deeply felt or recurring dreams. Watch for insights into what they might mean, and what you love doing.

It May Be Time
for a "Fill Year"

YOU DON'T HAVE TO WAIT TO DO WHAT YOU LOVE—YOU CAN TAKE WHAT
I call a "Fill Year," and start exploring your interests now.

No matter what obligations you may have, the goal of a Fill Year is to
explore as many of your interests as possible. The key to doing what you
love is making time each day to develop your strengths, and to express
your interests through your work or hobbies. Get out and try things.
Whatever interests you, pursue it.

At this point you may be wondering how you can possibly find the time
to do this in your busy life—with a full-time job and myriad responsibilities
to other people. So what can you do?

I did some homework and figured out that there are about eighteen
workweeks per year in which to explore your interests, if you plan carefully
and really focus. Here's a look at the math: You have thirty minutes at lunch
three times per week; thirty minutes at night three times per week; one
night per week; two weekend nights per month; two weekend days per
month; and one week of your annual vacation time to fill your year with
many meaningful activities.

How do you know what is fulfilling to you? Start by looking back at the
main periods in your life: childhood, high school, college, jobs, marriage,
children, and your career. When were you the happiest? When were you

the most successful? What were you doing? What were you learning? What activities did you enjoy? What were you reading? What were you writing? Who were you spending time with? Your answers to these questions will help uncover your passions in life.

Search

HOW ELSE CAN YOU FIND CLUES TO WHAT YOU LOVE TO DO? ASK THE PEOPLE in your life what they think. What have they seen you do well? What have you expressed an interest in? Ask your family, friends, and coworkers. Their insights might surprise you.

If you don't know which activities are available to you, check event calendars, or call local universities, museums, libraries, theaters, concert halls, hotels, chambers of commerce, local governments, and houses of worship. Find out which associations have chapters in your area. Get a listing of local clubs. See what's interesting to you, and start plugging activities into your calendar.

Some of you may be thinking that you really can't take this amount of time away from your spouse, children, parents, friends, or coworkers. This is where you play "Fill Year Matchmaking." Think about who might be willing to participate in some of the activities that you find interesting, and then invite them to go along with you. They'll appreciate the invitation; you'll do something fun together; and you'll have taken another step forward in your year of exploration.

Second Promise Actions

PULL OUT YOUR PLANNER AND BEGIN SCHEDULING ACTIVITIES THAT YOU find interesting. Do something every day that helps you better understand what ignites your passion.

How to Keep Your Job During Your Fill Year

ANDY ROONEY, JOURNALIST AND TELEVISION COMMENTATOR, IS CREDITED with saying, "I've learned that everyone wants to live on top of the mountain, but all the happiness and growth occurs while you're climbing it."

Research by the University of Pennsylvania psychologist Martin Seligman has demonstrated that when people have the opportunity to use their natural strengths, experience positive emotion, and engage in meaningful activities, they are happy. Seligman's research points to the importance of the voyage of life, not just the final port of call.

In a Fill Year, you explore the activities that engage your strengths, and the activities that are gratifying to you. Whatever interests you, pursue it.

But how do you explore your interests when you're working full-time? Start a Fill Year project at work. With a little planning and creativity, you can find opportunities to explore your interests with the blessing and support of your company. Here are a few strategies.

Consider how you might participate in company initiatives related to your interests. What events does your company sponsor that you could attend? What volunteer activities could you sign up for—or plan? Which task forces or committees could you join? Which training sessions could you attend; which ones could you lead? What party could you organize? What employee recognition event could you design? What educational session could you coordinate? Who could you mentor? What research could you conduct? What newsletter could you write? Which temporary assignments could you take?

Seek Them Out

FIND OUT WHO SHARES YOUR INTERESTS IN YOUR COMPANY. FORM GROUPS. Join organizations. Go to events together. At MasterCard I went to lectures after work with members of other departments. Our exploration together led to an even better partnership at work. What could you do with senior management? What could you do with your team?

Companies love to see their employees participate in team-building activities inside and outside of work. What fun and interesting activities would your company support? At Yahoo! I gave my employees a budget each month to plan events that brought our department together. What activities could you arrange?

Now, what if you're contemplating a new career or opening your own business? Follow my grandfather's advice. He used to say, "If you want to go into the stationery business, work in a stationery store." His message was to learn the business first then decide if you want to take the plunge. Use some of your Fill Year to work part time or volunteer in a business that you're interested in. Do it for the experience, not for the money.

Autotelic is my favorite "big" word. It means, "having an end or purpose in and not apart from itself." It comes from the Greek word *autotelis*, which translates to "complete in itself." Your Fill Year goal is to engage in as many autotelic experiences as possible: Choose activities that are meaningful to you, no matter where they might take you.

One of the seminars I went to when I was working for MasterCard was called "How to Write Professionally." I thought it would be interesting. Twenty years later, my books are now published in twelve languages.

Follow your interests—you never know where they will take you.

Second Promise Actions

YOUR TASK REMAINS THE SAME: PULL OUT YOUR PLANNER AND BEGIN scheduling the activities listed above. Do something every day at work that helps you better understand what ignites your passion.

Let Other People Teach You

WHEN I WAS SEVENTEEN YEARS OLD, I THOUGHT I WANTED TO BE AN orthopedic surgeon, so I took advantage of an offer to shadow the Milwaukee Brewers' baseball team doctor. I expected to watch surgeries and meet baseball players, but I had a different experience.

There were no surgeries to watch. There were no baseball stadiums to visit. There were only examination-room doors to open and close. We visited patients in the surgeon's office all day long—more than I can remember. I knew the visits were important (my own orthopedic doctors had helped me many times), and I enjoyed meeting new people—I just didn't realize how much of a doctor's week was spent in the office bouncing from room to room. I learned in one week that the path of a doctor was not for me.

Who will you observe this year to test your interests? Don't romanticize an interest; investigate it.

Let other people teach you. Learn by asking others, and don't be constrained by going it alone: Meet with people who love what they do in your company (your interest will make them feel appreciated); ask them what excites them about their work, how they discovered their passion, and what they did to get where they are in their career. You will learn a lot about yourself as you listen to their stories, and you will also expand and deepen your relationships as a result.

Lunch

WHEN I WAS AT YAHOO! ONE OF THE MANY PEOPLE I RESPECTED AND admired was Kirk Froggatt, former VP of Human Resources. Kirk loved any activity that helped inspire and develop Yahoo! employees. One day I joined him for lunch. At the time I was running Yahoo!'s Customer Care division.

We talked for two hours. Over the ensuing months, I read Kirk's white papers, plans, and recommended books. I loved everything he sent to me, and along the way I discovered that my true path was in the field of learning and development. One year later, I moved into a full-time role leading the training organization at Yahoo! It started with a lunch.

Who will you meet with this year? Be humble. Reach out.

Learn by the example of others.

Determination

IN 1917, MY GRANDFATHER LIVED IN BRUNSWICK, MAINE. AT THE AGE OF twenty-three, he worked as a bookkeeper for the Bath Iron Works, the largest shipbuilder in the United States at the time. He worked long hours, had little extra money, and lived at home. He had only an elementary school education, but he dreamed of becoming an accountant.

Despite his circumstances, my grandfather found a way to pursue his dream. He adhered to a motto: "I can. I will." He borrowed the correspondence course books that his older brother had purchased years earlier to study accounting. He set aside two hours every night after work to read the books and take the practice tests (without looking at his brother's answers). My grandfather would then clear his mind with a walk, and then go to bed. For two years he followed this plan. In 1919, my grandfather passed the state of Maine and the state of New Hampshire accounting exams.

The original certificate conferring my grandfather's right to practice accounting hangs in my parent's family room. It reminds my family of what you can achieve when you make the time to pursue your passion.

Whose example will you emulate this year? Learn from their journey. Discover your path.

Second Promise Actions

MAKE A LIST OF ALL THE PEOPLE WHO COULD TEACH YOU. THEN, START making Second Promise plans to do what is necessary to meet with them.

Tell People Your Dreams

CONSIDER THIS. YOU'RE AT A PARTY AND SOMEONE SAYS, "WHAT ARE YOU UP to?" How would you respond? Most of the time we fumble through our answers. We say things like, "Not much. Business is good. Family's good. How about you?"

Why waste time boring yourself and others with responses like these. Let other people know what you love to do; ask for their ideas and advice. Most people will feel closer to you as a result. And those who show no interest in your passion are better left alone; there's no need to spend much time with people who do not care about what matters to you.

It's time to break the thinking that it's okay to keep your dreams locked up inside. Why put a harness on your life? Waiting to pursue what you love is not a requirement of life. And you don't have to wait for the perfect time to share your dreams.

Share Your Passion

HERE'S HOW I LIKE TO RESPOND TO THE QUESTION, "WHAT ARE YOU UP TO?" I say, "I'm excited about writing my next book." Then I pause and give them time to respond. If they express interest, I like to thank them for the encouragement and follow with a question I'm thinking about. I say something such as, "You know, I'd love your thoughts on something." I open myself to their feedback and give them a chance to contribute.

Then I return the favor and ask them what they are focusing on. I try to engage them, and I offer my help.

Heidi Goff, former MasterCard Division General Manager once told me, "Always come ready with your paperwork to be signed." Her point was that you should believe in your work enough that you are ready for someone to sign on the bottom line at any time.

Goff's advice also applies to meeting people. You should be ready to share your passion with others. People may be ready to help you right now. Give them the opportunity.

Trust Yourself

TRUST YOURSELF TO KNOW THAT YOU ARE COMMITTED TO YOUR DREAMS, that your desire to change your life is sincere. Don't get caught up in an inner dialogue that questions your commitment. It won't help you to repeat, "I'm not sure if I really want to do this or not, so I better not say anything." And what if your dreams change? Great. Share them too. They'll always be interesting.

Trust that your dreams are real. While you might not yet have a plan to make your dreams a reality, believe in yourself and trust that they'll come true.

Second Promise Actions

LOOK AT YOUR CALENDAR. WHERE WILL YOU BE THIS MONTH? WHERE IS IT likely that people will ask you how you're doing and what you're up to? Make it a 3 Promises activity to answer these questions with thoughtful, informative updates. When people ask you what you're doing, answer them with confidence and enthusiasm.

The Rule of the Test Drive

SIXTEEN YEARS AGO IN AN AUTOMOBILE SHOWROOM, I LEARNED A powerful lesson from advice my grandfather had given me: "Try out your interests before judging them or committing to them." The experience was a powerful reminder that dreams unexplored are nothing more than untested ideas.

For years, I'd had my eyes on one car—a red convertible. I loved everything about it, even though I'd never driven it: The shape of the body was unique; the black fabric on top looked great; and the glossy body paint was perfect.

In 1997, when I moved from New York to Atlanta, I needed a car. I thought, "Why not get the car I liked so much."

So I did some research. An Atlanta dealership had just the one I wanted. My girlfriend, Dawn—now my wife of fifteen years—came with me.

We arrived at the lot. I loved the car as soon as I saw it. A salesman came out to meet us, and then we sat down at his desk to talk about how unique and attractive the car was.

Then I started negotiating. We talked about the sale price, financing, and warranties. We talked a lot. A little further along in the conversation, the salesman stepped away to get some more information.

Dawn's Advice

DAWN WATCHED THE SALESMAN UNTIL HE WAS OUT OF HEARING RANGE. She leaned in to me and said, "Why don't you take the car for a test drive?"

I laughed. "Why hadn't I thought of that?" I was so caught up in talking about the car; I had forgotten the most important thing. When the salesman returned, I asked him if I could take the car for a spin.

"Okay," he said. "Let me get the keys."

We went out to the lot. I opened the car door excitedly and slipped into the driver's seat. I was about to drive my dream car. Dawn sat up front with me, while the salesman settled into the back.

I turned on the car. The motor was louder than I'd expected. I drove out of the parking lot and put my foot on the accelerator to merge with the traffic on a busy street. The pickup was slower than I'd anticipated. We turned onto the highway. As I continued to drive the car, I couldn't help noticing that it just wasn't as comfortable as I'd expected. When we returned to the lot, Dawn and I got out of the car and stepped to the side.

"What did you think?" Dawn said.

"The car is beautiful, but it doesn't drive or feel like I thought it would," I said.

"What are you going to do?"

"I'm not going to buy it. It looks great, but it's not the car I want to drive every day."

After all those years of admiration and all that talk in the showroom, it took only a ten-minute test drive to make me see that the car was not for me.

Have you experienced this yourself at some point? You dream about something for years, only to realize that you're still sitting in the showroom. All you really need is a good "test drive."

Many of us experience showroom dreams with our careers. We say things like, "That's what I'd really like to do," or "If I were doing that, I would be so happy." Then you look at what you're currently doing and realize that you're not spending any time exploring your dreams. They're so "in your head" that you don't take any action. You debate with yourself and others, but you don't step forward. You're stuck in the showroom just thinking about what you want, what you would enjoy, and what you would be good at doing.

This is exactly when you need to follow "The Rule of the Test Drive": If something interests you, walk out onto the lot, and take your interest for a ride.

The Rule of the Test Drive will also help you get away from the "ifs": "If I were given the opportunity. If I were discovered. If I had more luck. If I had less responsibility at work and at home. If I had more time, money, support. If only I didn't have these constraints, I'd pursue the life I want to lead."

When you slide into the driver's seat and turn the key in the ignition, you'll quickly find out one of three things. 1. You like what you're exploring, and you want to do more of it. 2. You don't like it, and you'd rather put your energy somewhere else. 3. You're not sure if you like it, and you need to give it another try.

Whatever the result, at least you're making a genuine (and, I would say, a courageous) effort to explore your interests. Ultimately, you are moving yourself closer to doing what you love.

Second Promise Actions

IF YOU'VE BEEN "SURE" ABOUT WANTING TO PURSUE SOMETHING THAT interests you, but have not yet created an opportunity to try it out, now is the time. Think about ways you can take your interest out for a test drive. Schedule these Second Promise activities as soon as possible.

Take "The Morning Test™"

IT HAD BEEN A LONG DAY AT WORK, AND I WAS TIRED. IT WAS ALMOST 10:00 p.m. Dawn and the girls were in bed, and I was headed for the couch. I needed to watch TV—I had to relax before bedtime. I deserved it.

And then the next morning I woke up tired. I was so tired that I woke up thinking about going to bed that night. It was obvious that I needed more sleep. Yet every night I "needed" to relax on the couch. I lived this stay-up-late, wake-up-tired cycle for a long time. The obvious connection between my choices at night and how I felt in the morning was something I never fully admitted to myself until I took what I call, "The Morning Test™."

Here's how the test works. Every night for one week, write down everything that you do at night. Jot down what you eat for snacks, the TV shows you watch, the radio programs you listen to, the email you read, the sites you surf, and whatever else you do.

Then, immediately after waking up the next morning—and this is important—think about what you did the night before. Think about everything you did that makes you feel fulfilled and what you think was a waste of time. Write it all down.

Evaluate

AFTER WRITING DOWN ALL OF YOUR NIGHTTIME ACTIVITIES FOR ONE WEEK, make a note of which activities help you fulfill the 3 Promises, and which ones don't. It'll give you an opportunity to replace some of your less helpful habits with activities that lead to more joy in your life, doing more of what you love to do, and making a meaningful contribution to others.

Why is this important? Because we always wish we had more time to do more of what we care about. This exercise will help you make sure that what you do at night serves you well the next day and helps you achieve the important goals in your life. It's hard to focus on developing your interests, expanding your knowledge, and building experience in the career of your dreams when you constantly feel deprived of time. If you feel your time is scarce, you are less likely to give it away in the service of others. However, when you realize you have ample time to help others, your giving goes up significantly. Most of us are afraid to change our habits, especially those at nighttime. We feel powerful emotions, believing that we "deserve" to watch TV, or that we've earned the right to just "veg out." We think we'll feel cheated the next day if we don't indulge ourselves.

I asked Ed Diener, a leading happiness researcher, about the staying power of our nighttime emotions. Diener told me that his research shows that 95 percent of the emotions we experience before bedtime dissipate by the morning. When you take The Morning Test you realize that the emotional need you felt to do certain things at night, before bed, is mostly gone when you wake up. It would seem that most of our emotions are reset each morning.

Change

THE MORNING TEST HELPS JUMP–START CHANGE IN OUR LIVES. IF YOU FIND yourself headed to the couch tonight with a remote control in one hand and a dessert in the other, take The Morning Test when you wake up tomorrow. It could lead to an important and lasting change in your life: You may discover that you actually have more time to do what you love.

Second Promise Actions

TAKE THE MORNING TEST EACH DAY THIS WEEK. WRITE DOWN WHAT YOU discover. What opportunities do you have to spend more time on activities you truly love?

A New Way to Say "Yes"

TOO OFTEN WE SAY "YES" WHEN WE REALLY WANT TO SAY "NO." SOMEONE makes a request of you, and you feel pressured to accept it. You may face this situation practically every week, if not every day—and the request can be any flavor: "Will you join the committee?" "Will you serve on the board?" "Will you lead the project?" "Will you come to the party?"

Invariably, the people making a request are sincere and committed to what they're doing, and they're recruiting you because of the value you'll bring to their initiative. It's hard to say "no" when they ask. And if they're someone who is really persuasive, persistent, or aggressive, it's even harder to say "no." The challenge—no matter how effective or pressure-filled the request—is that you only have so much time and energy to give.

When I ask the people I coach, or the audiences in my seminars and speeches, how much they enjoy saying "no," the answer is always "not very much." So, I teach them how to say "yes" to their own priorities and projects, rather than putting excess energy into their "nos." I explain that when you say you are not able to join another committee or start another activity, for example, you are saying "yes" to something else in your life; it could be more time with your family, coaching your children's sports, exercising, writing your book, or any number of *your* priorities. You just have to politely say "no" because of the other commitments you have (how much you share about those commitments depends on the relationship). When you are working to advance your passion to do what you love, you have to be deliberate about how you spend your time.

Relief

THIS NEW WAY OF SAYING "YES" RELIEVES YOU OF THE HEAVY BURDEN THAT is often associated with having to say "no." And while others might be disappointed with your decision, they will respect the clarity of your commitment to the things that are important to you.

When you say "yes" to your life, you are building confidence to set and follow your own course. You are not tied to the direction that others prefer that you take. Saying "yes" to what matters most in your life makes it possible for you to save time to feel joy, pursue the career of your choice, and help others in ways that are meaningful.

Second Promise Actions

WHAT REQUESTS HAVE BEEN MADE OF YOU THAT YOU STILL NEED TO answer? And what requests are you expecting? Use the new way of saying "yes" to help you choose the answer you prefer without feeling guilty.

Get the Backstory of Success

WHEN WE LEARN ABOUT HOW SOME PEOPLE HAVE BECOME FAMOUS AND successful, we usually feel that what they have achieved is out of our reach: They are too accomplished, too far ahead of us, and we say to ourselves that we could never achieve what they have done. But this thinking is not helpful either to us or the people in our lives.

When you get caught up in the headlines of other people's success, instead of the backstory of their achievements, it's easy to get down on yourself. You see the goals reached but not the paths taken. You see the celebration but not the hard work and determination.

When you draw negative conclusions about your future, without proper research, planning, and effort, you put unnecessary obstacles in your way. Life is challenging enough without putting ungrounded limitations on yourself.

Thankfully, you can get beyond the headlines of success and read people's actual stories—their biographies, memoirs, and autobiographies. You can learn how to increase your success and fulfill your mission by studying someone else's journey.

I recently read *The Autobiography of Martin Luther King Jr.*, edited by Clayborne Carson. It's a wonderful book about an incredible man. While I was amazed by everything he had accomplished, his story reminded me that his journey did not begin on the mountaintop. It started in his father's church and in his neighborhood—and it continued in college, in graduate school, and when he chose his first church to pastor. His leadership in the civil rights movement began one event at a time. You may not be destined to change the world as profoundly as King, but you can learn to apply the lessons of his life to yours and achieve great things.

Get the backstory of success, and move closer to doing what you love.

Second Promise Actions

CONSIDER THE FIELD YOU ARE PASSIONATE ABOUT. WHO DO YOU HOLD IN high regard? Who has had the kind of success you would like for yourself? Make a plan for discovering their backstory.

Change Your Seat and Come to Life

FOURTEEN YEARS AGO I ATTENDED A THREE-DAY LEADERSHIP CONFERENCE in San Francisco. I arrived a few minutes early the first morning. There must have been a hundred people in the room, many of whom were already sitting in their seats or drinking coffee at the back of the room. But everyone had staked a claim on a seat for the day. There was just one chair left, so I grabbed a cup of coffee and sat down.

The first day of the conference was good, and it was interesting to talk with the people around my table.

Day Two

ON THE SECOND DAY OF THE CONFERENCE, I LEFT THE HOUSE A LITTLE earlier so that I could sit in another part of the room and meet new people. The roads were pretty clear that morning, and I arrived thirty minutes ahead of time. I put my bag down on a seat, at a new table, and went to the back of the room to get a cup of coffee.

Watching people arrive, I noticed that they were returning to the same seats that they had been sitting in the day before. I thought it was a bit curious, but I kept to my coffee and conversation. When it was time to take our seats, I looked around as I walked to my chair. It seemed everyone in the room was sitting in the same seat as the first day of the conference—except for two people, that is: me and a young woman who was glaring at me for taking her seat. Out of 100 people, apparently I was the only one who changed his seat on purpose.

As I had planned, I learned a lot from the people around my new table. I had another good day.

Day Three

DAY THREE CAME, AND MY PLAN WAS THE SAME: I LEFT EARLY FROM HOME so that I could arrive in time to choose a seat in yet another part of the conference room. Unfortunately, traffic that morning was bumper to bumper; my buffer time was lost on the highway. I arrived with five minutes to spare before the session started.

I ran up the hotel stairs and opened the door to our meeting room. Everyone in the room was back in the seat they had chosen on day one, including the unhappy young woman whose seat I had taken the day before. She was smiling at me as I settled into my original seat.

At that moment I was reminded how often we choose comfort over change. We prefer to stay in the same familiar seat in life rather than risk meeting new people and trying new things.

Most people sit in the same seat and expect life to come to them. Be different. Change your seat and you will come to life.

Be willing to change your perspective. Be interested in other people and open to new ideas. The most successful people I know constantly challenge themselves. They talk to people with different ideas and they try new things. They do what they love and they enjoy personal growth.

So my question is, "Where are you sitting?" Or, more to the point, "When are you going to change your seat?"

Second Promise Actions

LOOK AT YOUR MEETING AND EVENT SCHEDULE OVER THE NEXT MONTH. Keep in mind your mission to do what you love, and make plans to meet new people. Expand your learning. Extend yourself. Make new connections.

27

"What's Your Story?!"

"WHAT'S YOUR STORY?!" WE USED TO ASK THAT QUESTION WHEN I WAS growing up in Wisconsin. We didn't know what the question really meant; it was more of an expression. We just wanted to know why people were acting the way they were.

More Than "Facts"

DURING MY FRESHMAN YEAR IN COLLEGE, I WAS ASKED TO PLAY A SIMPLE game in an introductory psychology class. Professor Judith Rodin (future president of the University of Pennsylvania), asked us to be an "eyewitness" to a staged event and describe what we saw afterward. You can guess the results. Descriptions of the same event differed from student to student—sometimes dramatically. The facts were not as obvious as we thought they would be.

Similarly, the story of a life isn't easily captured in a list of events. Our lives are based mostly on a set of interpretations we have made about events in our lives. These interpretations add up to a story—the story of who we think we are, what we have experienced, and what we're likely to do in the future.

The psychologist Shane Lopez, a leading authority on the psychology of hope, points to the central role our stories play in our lives. Lopez writes in his book, *Making Hope Happen*, "Each time we retrieve a memory, we tend to revise or edit it, adding some new elements to the story and taking away others. In time, we decide that certain stories are representative of who we are and who we want to become. We rehearse them and we may share them with others. And we look to these stories for emotional guidance."

If your story includes doing what you love, many opportunities will be open to you. The passion you demonstrate will attract others to support your work and hobbies.

An "Adventure" Story

A FEW YEARS AGO I WENT WITH MY MOM TO AN ART HISTORY CLASS AT Florida Atlantic University. The lecturer that day was Professor David Courtney. The room was packed. Courtney's message to the class was captured in one question: "Are you taking an adventure every day of your life?" He asked us to immerse ourselves in something we love, something that challenges us, every day.

Each day is an opportunity to build a positive life story. Your story guides your actions; it is the link to realizing your best possible life.

The psychologist Dan McAdams refers to our stories as our personal myths. McAdams writes, "If you feel that your myth is stagnant, if you sense that you are not moving forward in life with purpose, if you believe that you are falling behind in some sense with respect to the growth of your personal identity, then what you are looking for is developmental change in personal myth." In other words, you need to change your story.

Consider Courtney's advice. Consider McAdams' advice, and write your story. Just make sure it includes doing what you love.

Second Promise Actions

REMEMBER THE 3 PROMISES STORY YOU ARE CREATING FOR YOURSELF. YOU have committed to Find Joy Every Day, Do What You Love, and Make a Difference. Expand your story to include what you're doing right now and what you will be doing to live the 3 Promises.

To Predict Your Future,
Look at Your Beliefs

MY FAVORITE MOVIE WHEN I WAS GROWING UP WAS *HEAVEN CAN WAIT* (1978), with Warren Beatty and Julie Christie. The premise of the movie is that "Joe Pendleton" (played by Beatty), a backup quarterback, wants to lead his football team, the Los Angeles Rams, to the Super Bowl. Early on in the movie, he goes for a ride on his bicycle on a remote highway. The camera shows him peacefully riding into a mountain tunnel. Then the frame expands to show the other side of the tunnel, where a car is recklessly passing another car on the wrong side of the road. Moments later Beatty and the oncoming cars (clearly on a collision course) are hidden inside the mountain. We are left with a view of the mountain and the sound of a horrific accident.

The next scene shows a bewildered Beatty, as he slowly realizes that he's in a transfer station waiting to go to heaven. The problem is that Beatty is not supposed to die. He is supposed to survive the accident. Unfortunately, an overzealous angel played by Buck Henry, mistakenly plucks Beatty from Earth. Henry's heavenly boss, played by James Mason, sets out to correct the mistake by helping Joe find his way back to life. The challenge is that they have to find someone who is about to die and then place Joe in that person's body. The idea is that Joe would then have to live the rest of his life in the new body. Joe's problem is that he has to achieve his goals in the body and life of another person.

Our Beliefs

HERE'S WHAT CAPTIVATED ME ABOUT THE MOVIE—THE IDEA THAT OUR beliefs direct our lives. If you believe that you can do something, and you are determined to do it, you can achieve great things. While Joe inherited someone's body, life, and relationships, his character and his beliefs were still his. After Joe comes back to life, he is intent on returning to professional football, no matter what it takes: His conviction transcends the body and life he occupies. So, it is no surprise at the end of the movie that . . . (I'll let you watch the movie to find out for yourself). I'll just say that Joe's beliefs are critical to his success.

Your beliefs and desires underlie your behavior. If you want to know what you are going to achieve in your life, you must find out what your deep-down, unconscious beliefs are.

Second Promise Actions

START IDENTIFYING YOUR BELIEFS. WHICH ONES ARE HELPING YOU BRING OUT your best? Which of your beliefs are outdated or limiting you? Be honest with yourself. Unlike Warren Beatty in *Heaven Can Wait,* you have only one body you can count on to do what you love.

Build Your Own Case for Success, and Believe in It

A NUMBER OF YEARS AGO I WAS AT A DINNER PARTY. A SMALL GROUP OF us were standing in the hall when a friend turned to me and said, "How's your book coming?"

"Almost done . . . just editing," I said.

"Do you have a publisher?"

"One of the New York publishers is reviewing my book proposal and manuscript."

Then, one of the guests I met that night jumped in.

"It's tough to publish a book," he said. "Talk to John."

John was the host of the party—and busy introducing guests to each other in another room.

"What happened to John?" I said.

"He wrote a great book," the guest said. "I read it."

He paused for a sip of wine. He then slowly shook his head. "John had all the connections. He knew all the publishers. He knew all the agents. And he still couldn't get anyone to publish his book."

"That's too bad," I said.

"Yeah. I'm just telling you because it's hard."

"That's what I've heard." Then I asked, "Could John's book still be published?"

He said, "Oh yeah. It's great. Still timely."

"Maybe he could try again," I said.

"I don't know. The economy is terrible."

"Yeah, it's not good."

"Look at the layoffs at the publishing houses," he said. "It's not a good time to be coming out with a book."

He stopped as if he realized he was not being very encouraging.

He flashed a smile and said, "Well, I hope it goes well with your book."

Beliefs

THIS WAS NOT THE FIRST TIME I HAD HEARD SOMEONE PAINT A DARK scenario about publishing. I had heard other versions of the same story: It's not easy to publish a book. (In fact, it's not easy to write a book.) More people fail than succeed in the book-publishing business. The real question was, would I succeed or fail?

Here's the answer: It could go either way, depending on what I believed. If I focused on what John's friend was saying, I would convince myself that book publishing is hard (look at what happened to John). Even if I knew the right agents, publishers, and had a great story, I still might not get the book published. If the economy didn't improve, publishers would be less likely to spend money on a new book. The odds were against me.

Are these beliefs reasonable? Absolutely—each one is based in reality. The question is, "How often in our lives do we stop there?" Someone provides evidence for a belief—in conversation, on television, or in the newspaper—and we accept it. We back away from our dreams and we get "realistic."

I had a choice to make. Should I accept the assessments of others without challenging them, or should I build my own case for success? If I had any chance of succeeding, I would have to produce my own evidence to support a belief that my book would be published. And better yet, it would be successful.

Postscript

NOT LONG AFTER THAT DINNER PARTY, THE RIGHTS TO PUBLISH MY BOOK were bought by Sterling, a competitive New York publishing house. *The Law of the Garbage Truck* is now an international bestseller that has been translated into twelve languages.

Second Promise Actions

WHAT ABOUT YOU? IS ANYONE PRESENTING CREDIBLE ARGUMENTS AGAINST your dreams? Have people expressed reasonable doubts about your plans? What are you doing? Will you continue to move ahead and seek new evidence for your mission? Or will you be reasonable and stop pushing forward to achieve your dreams?

Go ahead and build your own evidence. Create your own case for success. Sure, you'll have days when doubt creeps in—especially after a setback—but you will quickly realize that a bump in the road does not mean failure. You are committed to success, and you believe it will happen. You can do it. Keep making it happen. Doing what you love is too important.

Don't Hold Yourself Back

IT CAN BE HARD ENOUGH TO PURSUE YOUR DREAMS IN THE FACE OF THE opinions, assessments, and advice from the people you care about, but it's a lot harder if you're worried about what everyone else could be thinking—especially if you think it might be negative. This focus on the opinions of others limits your self-expression and disrupts your productivity. A trip to New York City made this particularly clear to me.

It was 6:00 a.m., and I looked out my hotel window and saw at least seven buildings with forty floors or more. I wondered how many people would work in those buildings that day.

After I showered and dressed, I walked through Times Square. I looked around at all the people and thought, where is everyone going?

When I arrived at Grand Central Station, there were thousands of people in the station: They were getting off trains, boarding trains, and waiting for trains. I wondered what they did for a living and what their ambitions were.

I bought a muffin and a cup of coffee in the station, and I sat down on a bench. I watched everyone, and then it hit me: All the people I passed that day—and there were thousands of them—did not care about me, and they wouldn't have cared about you, either. This sounds harsh, but let me clarify what I mean.

Misplaced Worry

I BELIEVE THAT COUNTLESS PEOPLE WOULD HELP US IF WE WERE IN NEED. I also believe that many people care about us spiritually, and feel connected to us, even though we've never actually met. And I believe that people would be interested in us, if we did something extraordinary or broke the law. People are interested in us, and what we do, on many levels.

In practical terms, though, most people do not care about us, simply because they don't actually know us, or know us very well. Consequently, they are not invested in our lives and don't particularly care what we do for a living, what our dreams are, what we study, what we practice, or what we do every day.

When we are honest with ourselves, there are not many people in the world who focus their attention on us every day. People simply have to attend to their own lives to make them work; we do not have the luxury of worrying about someone we don't know very well, or at all.

Then why do most of us worry about "what other people think"? Most of us go about our lives worried about what "everyone else thinks" about our dreams, careers, finances, relationships, and work. We worry about failing in front of others. We worry about not being good enough or doing enough. We worry about looking bad.

Would we worry so much if we were guaranteed that our potential failures would be kept private?

Freedom

THE REALITY IS THAT WE PRACTICALLY HAVE THAT PRIVACY GUARANTEE already: Most of our successes and failures are unknown to the world. Only celebrities—movie, music, sports, and political stars—have their lives examined on a daily basis for everyone to see. The rest of us live in near anonymity.

This is good news. It means we have freedom. We have the flexibility to choose the path in life that is best for us. We can experiment. We can explore. We can live our best possible life.

Here's something else important to note. When people do become aware of our successes, they are mostly concerned with the results, not the journey. Some of us have to study harder, work longer hours, and make more mistakes along the way than the average person. Fortunately, all of that is forgotten when we succeed. The cameras flash when we are on the victory stand, not when we are on the practice field.

Second Promise Actions

THE NEXT TIME YOU WANT TO MAKE AN IMPORTANT CHANGE IN YOUR LIFE, and you are afraid of what "others" might think, take what I call the "New York City Test." Look outside your imaginary hotel window in New York City, walk through Times Square, stop in Grand Central Station, and count all the people that are worried about your life. Remind yourself that your success or failure is your concern and not the focus of the world.

Know that you are free. Do What You Love. Don't hold yourself back because of "what other people might think."

Don't Hide

IN HIGH SCHOOL, FOOTBALL WAS MY LIFE, AND BEING A FOOTBALL PLAYER was my identity. I helped my team win the conference championship for my school by scoring a fifty-five yard touchdown run, and I broke all our rushing records. And then, I was admitted to Yale University. I had a chance to play college football.

When I arrived at Yale's training camp, the coaches put the depth chart of each position on the locker room wall. I walked over, looked up, and saw that I was eighth on the depth chart at running back. I couldn't believe it. I had always been the starter. Now, I was the backup guy to the seventh guy.

I worked as hard as anyone on the team to rise in the ranks, and one week prior to the start of the season, I became the backup to the starter. In our first game of the season, I was given the ball once for a run. I ran for seven yards. It wasn't much, but it was a start.

The next week was better. The coaches gave me an opportunity to go head-to-head with the starter in practice. He would run a play. I would run a play. That day I happened to be playing my best football ever; then I ran a play that began the rest of my life.

The Play

THE QUARTERBACK MADE THE CALL AT THE LINE, THE CENTER SNAPPED THE ball, and I took off running. I needed to unleash a good block; I had to show the coaches how tough I was. I approached my target. I fixed my eyes on him. As I began to uncoil and deliver my block, I heard and felt a pop in my right leg. In an instant my hamstring retracted into a ball of muscle. I fell to the ground clutching my leg. Worse than the pain, I realized that my season could be over.

I wouldn't give up. I did everything the trainers asked me to do. Three weeks after my injury, my trainers told me I was ready to sprint and start playing again. I didn't think so; there was a tightness deep inside my leg that I couldn't quite loosen up. The trainers knew better—it was their job—so, I did what they said.

They told me, "Start jogging."

I did.

They yelled, "Start running."

I did.

They hollered, "Sprint!"

I took one step with my good leg, and then as I started my stride with the injured leg, I heard the sound of a giant rubber band snapping. I came crashing down. I knew it immediately: My season was over.

I still wouldn't give up. I was a football player, and I had to play football. I spent the rest of my freshman year rehabilitating my hamstring. I got myself into the best playing shape of my life.

One week before my sophomore football season, I was working out on a high school track. I had one more sprint in my workout. I stepped up to the starting line and took off flying down the track. When I was just steps from the finish line, I felt that pop again. I grabbed my hamstring and fell to the track. I knew it then: My football career was over.

Identity

FOR WEEKS I WANTED TO HIDE. I RAN ONE FOOTBALL PLAY FOR SEVEN YARDS in college. That was it. That was my career. I didn't want to face anyone. I worried that people would think I was a failure. I had been a football player all my life. Now who was I?

Many of us face questions of identity, and most are significantly more difficult than the one I faced thirty years ago. Everyone reels from unplanned and unwanted events. Life is hard when you get hurt, sick, divorced, laid off, fired, or when you lose money.

You may feel as though the whole world is watching you fail. But we already know the good news: People aren't really watching. They are thinking about their own challenges. It's only our closest family, friends, and colleagues who are concerned about us: They just want us to be happy, healthy, and successful. That's even better news. With their support, we don't need to hide.

We can create a new path in life.

Second Promise Actions

IF YOU'RE WORKING THROUGH A TRANSITION IN YOUR LIFE, USE THE SECOND Promise to help you create a new path with daily actions. Start with tomorrow. Plan something, do it, and then continue the next day, and keep going.

Step by step, you'll create the path of your dreams.

Your Success and Rocket Science

WHEN YOU WATCH COMMERCIALS ON TELEVISION, LISTEN TO PROMOTIONS on the radio, flip through magazine ads, and read marketing emails, you are constantly told that you're missing out: You could be making lots of money by working only a few hours a week, buying special products that are available for a limited time, or taking a weekend seminar. You're told that the path to greatness and having everything you want in life can be had almost overnight.

Yet, you know in your heart that success is not achieved this way. Success takes time. When you get away from all the marketing hype, you realize that sustained success comes to those who love what they do, feel that their work matters, and are committed to becoming experts in their field. During good times and bad times, we need to invest in what is meaningful and long-lasting.

Stephen King has sold more than 300 million books. One of his books, *On Writing*, is about the craft of writing and his journey as a writer. King's success is not a get-rich-quick story. He writes, "By the time I was fourteen (and shaving twice a week whether I needed to or not) the nail in my wall would no longer support the weight of the rejection slips impaled upon it. I replaced the nail with a spike and went on writing."

The next time you're being seduced by a shortcut-to-success message, think of Stephen King's journey to 300 million books sold.

Your Plans

WHEN YOU GIVE UP BELIEVING THAT THERE'S AN OVERNIGHT PATH TO success, you're faced with the reality that achieving your dreams will require significant effort. And if you're just getting started, things can look complicated: There's so much to learn and do. This was the challenge I experienced when I decided to write my first book, *The Law of the Garbage Truck*. I was a businessman, a newspaper columnist, and a speaker; I knew very little about writing and publishing a book. I was overwhelmed at the start. Everything I needed to do felt daunting.

Then, something fortunate happened: I visited NASA's Kennedy Space Center with my family. We took the tours, visited the exhibits, walked inside a retired space shuttle, took a picture of the lunar rover—we did it all. On one of the tours, I learned that it took more than 400,000 people working together to get the first astronauts to the moon. More than 400,000 people. That's a lot of rocket scientists. When I heard that, I thought of the troubles I was having with my book. I realized that they weren't as complicated as I thought they were. My book would require a lot of work, but I could do it. I could succeed on my mission without rocket scientists.

Your mission to do more of what you love in life may not need rocket scientists, either. You can do it.

Second Promise Actions

THIS IS A GOOD TIME TO LOOK AT YOUR VISION AND PLANS. ARE THERE important aspects of your plan that seem too complicated for you to accomplish? What are they?

Write them down.

Pause.

Are they as complicated as you think? In all likelihood, there is an answer waiting for you. You just have to ask the right person. Make it a point tomorrow to begin networking for the answers you need.

The Great Depression
Success Formula

WHEN I WAS GROWING UP, MY GRANDFATHER BUMPA POLLAY LIVED WITH US. He frequently told us stories. One was about the founding of the family business. He proudly told us that he started the company with his two brothers in 1937, during the heart of the Great Depression in the United States. And they did well. Why? Bumpa said it was because they focused on what they could control, not on the dire state of the economy.

Bumpa's formula for success was to provide a quality product, find a territory in the country that needed it, hire motivated salespeople to represent it, design an offer that customers valued, and then knock on as many doors as possible to sell it. His deep-seated belief was that opportunities are always available, even if everyone else seems to believe that there are none.

So: What are your beliefs about our economic environment? Do you believe that there are still good business opportunities? Do you believe that people are still succeeding? If you believe that opportunities are out there—and people are still finding them—what's keeping you from believing that you, too, will be successful.

Despite the Circumstances

FOR SIXTY-ONE YEARS, OUR FAMILY BUSINESS THRIVED AND SURVIVED THE Great Depression, four wars, recessions, changing technology, and the arrival of megastores. Bumpa, and my father after him, had all the excuses that could weigh down a less determined company, such as, people don't have money (the Depression); workers are not available; materials are rationed or not available (World War II); customers aren't spending (recessions); competition is fierce (megastores); and so on. Bumpa's belief—and my father's, when he bought the business—was that while others were blaming and complaining about things beyond their power, he and his team had an opportunity to keep on selling. Distractions he could not control did not deter him.

The challenge for us is to not let issues such as tough competition, difficult customers, lack of support, too much paperwork, complex products, long sales cycles, high sales quotas, and a depressed economy convince us that we cannot succeed. While it is natural to be concerned, even fearful, when facing these challenges, we cannot let the factors beyond our control determine our success. The easy way out is to give in and start believing that we cannot succeed in a difficult economic environment.

The better thing for us to do is to get into a joyful, creative, curious, open-minded, grateful, and optimistic state every day. It will enable us to build better relationships with our customers and partners. It will allow us to see how we can make the most of our company's products, services, and support systems to meet the needs of our customers.

The father of modern psychology, William James, said, "The world we see that seems so insane is the result of a belief system that is not working. To perceive the world differently, we must be willing to change our belief system, let the past slip away, expand our sense of now, and dissolve the fear in our minds."

When you read the news each morning, and when people state opinions, remind yourself to follow Bumpa's advice:

Believe you have opportunities.

Look for them and develop them.

Your desire to Do What You Love is too important to stop because things look hard.

Second Promise Actions

DO YOU SEE OBSTACLES TO ACHIEVING YOUR DREAMS? WHAT ARE THEY? List them, and then work on a plan to get past them. When you're pursuing your passion, there is always a way around the difficulties on your path.

Lay Down Your Towel

MY DAD TOLD ME A STORY THIRTY-SIX YEARS AGO THAT INSPIRED ME TO strive for excellence in all that I love, and to overcome any obstacles put in my path. It's the story of Jesse Owens, one of the greatest athletes in American history.

Jesse Owens, an African American track star from Ohio State University, was competing in the long jump at the 1936 Olympics in Nazi Germany. One of the competitors was Luz Long—a blond, blue-eyed athlete from Germany. Hitler desperately wanted Long to win the event in order to validate his propaganda for the superiority of the Aryan "master" race.

Owens had to jump a qualifying distance of twenty-four and a half feet to make it to the long jump finals. Before the official start of the competition, he took a practice jump in his warm-up clothes. Afterward, as he stepped out of the sand pit, the judges raised a red flag: They were counting Owens's practice jump as his first official attempt. After all the reports he had heard of Germany's hatred of Jews and blacks, Owens couldn't help but jump to the conclusion that the German officials were bent on ensuring a victory for Long.

Then it was Long's turn. He took the jump and qualified easily. Owens knew that the qualifying jump to make it to the next round was an easy one for him—he was the reigning world record holder—but he feared that the officials would take victory away from him with a bad call. On his second attempt, Owens was extra cautious. This time he crossed the line, drawing a second red flag from the judges.

The Jump

OWENS WAS DOWN TO ONE LAST ATTEMPT AT THE QUALIFYING DISTANCE TO make it into the finals with Long. As he kneeled in thought before his last jump, Long approached him. He put his hand on Owens's shoulder, looked at him, and told him to jump a half-foot behind the take-off board. If he did this, according to Long's advice, Owens would eliminate the possibility that an official could disqualify him for fouling. Long then put his towel on the exact spot from which Owens should jump.

Owens left the towel in place. He then took off down the runway for his final qualifying attempt. When he reached the towel, Owens planted his foot right behind it in plain view of the judges and jumped. He landed, watched the officials measure his jump, looked up at the judges, and waited with everyone for the news: He made it! Owens had set an unofficial world record.

The day of the finals, Owens and Long battled for the win. On Long's final jump of the day, he broke the world record and was one step away from the gold medal. Owens had just one more jump to beat Long's record and win the competition. He readied himself for his final jump, then sprinted down the runway and leapt high into the air. And to the astonishment of everyone in the stadium, Owens landed nearly six inches beyond Long's final jump: He had set a new world record and earned the gold medal for the United States.

Dad's story about Jesse Owens taught me to never leave my success to someone else's judgment.

Know what you love to do.

Know your passion.

Know the measure of your success.

Then, lay down your towel and jump.

Second Promise Actions

WHAT DOES SUCCESS ON YOUR PATH TO DOING WHAT YOU LOVE LOOK LIKE for you? What are the measures of your success? Review your plans, and make sure to lay down your towel. Be ambitious, and set your targets so failure is not an option.

T.H.E.
K.E.Y. T.E.S.T.™
of Doing What You Love

T.H.E. K.E.Y. T.E.S.T. WILL HELP YOU UNDERSTAND TO WHAT DEGREE YOU ARE fulfilling the Second Promise. The test is a ten-point guide to help you focus your strengths, passion, and resources on doing what you love.

FOR EACH OF THE TEN DIMENSIONS ON THE FOLLOWING PAGE, RATE yourself on a scale of "1 to 5." A "5" means that you're at the top of the dimension, and a "1" means that you're rated low in the dimension.

T.H.E. K.E.Y. T.E.S.T. of Doing What You Love

T. 1. I am **thinking** all the time about new ideas I can introduce and creative opportunities I can pursue in my chosen career.
1 2 3 4 5

H. 2. I have many people in my life who mentor and advise me. I do not hesitate to ask for **help**.
1 2 3 4 5

E. 3. I feel that my work makes a positive difference in the world. My **ethics** and values are in harmony with my contribution.
1 2 3 4 5

K. 4. I am an expert in my field. I am constantly reading, researching, and studying to build my **knowledge**.
1 2 3 4 5

E. 5. I seek as much **experience** as possible to deepen my ability to contribute personally and professionally. I continue to learn.
1 2 3 4 5

Y. 6. I **yearn** for the opportunity to do even more of my work. I want to find more ways of doing what I love.
1 2 3 4 5

T. 7. I am eager to **try** new things. I am willing to experiment to learn.
1 2 3 4 5

E. 8. I am **energized** by my life. My battery is continually charging.
1 2 3 4 5

S. 9. I use my most natural **strengths** every day. I get to do what I do best.
1 2 3 4 5

T. 10. I frequently participate in **training**. I am on the lookout for new insights and approaches to doing what I love even better.
1 2 3 4 5

Scoring T.H.E. K.E.Y. T.E.S.T. of Doing What You Love

ADD YOUR SCORES FROM THE TEN DIMENSIONS OF T.H.E. K.E.Y. T.E.S.T. OF Doing What You Love. Write your total score in the box below.

The Key

LOCATE YOUR SCORE BELOW TO FIND OUT HOW MUCH YOU ARE ACTIVELY engaged in doing what you love.

A SCORE BETWEEN 40 AND 50 INDICATES THAT YOU ARE ENGAGING, OR nearly engaging, the full power of your natural strengths personally and professionally. You are giving your best effort. You are on the right path. You love your career. You seek advice, help, and coaching to improve your life. You look for learning and training opportunities to advance your knowledge. You seek new experiences to test and to build your skills. Congratulations. Keep it up.

A SCORE BETWEEN 30 AND 39 INDICATES THAT YOU ARE NOT FULLY tapping your gifts. Work on recrafting your work, family, and community responsibilities to better align your activities with your natural strengths and passions. Redouble your effort to build your knowledge. Be open to advice, and seek help when you need it. Use the tools and strategies in this book to help you take your life to the next level. Your success will increase as a result.

A SCORE BETWEEN 20 AND 29 INDICATES THAT YOU ARE UNDERPERFORMING in important areas of your life. It's time to reevaluate your commitments. Get into action, and take on the Second Promise actions suggested at the end of each chapter. You will not succeed at the highest level if your heart and mind are not in it. You will reach your potential only if you tap your strengths and give your best effort personally and professionally.

A SCORE BETWEEN 0 AND 19 INDICATES THAT YOU ARE LIKELY IN A RUT personally and professionally. You will increase your success the more you are able to use your natural strengths every day. You will be on your way to fulfillment the more you are energized by what you do, the more you yearn to do what you love to do, and the more you feel that your work is meaningful. Take your time and implement the strategies in this book to increase your joy, passion, and meaning in life. You can do it. Take action and have faith.

PART 3

Make a Difference

*"Since you get more joy out of giving joy
to others, you should put a good deal of thought
into the happiness that you are able to give."*

—Eleanor Roosevelt

Start small. Just start. Don't limit yourself because of an imagined standard. Don't compare yourself to others. Commit to giving to others without a measuring stick.

Smile at someone. Laugh with someone. Show appreciation for someone. Forgive inconsequential mistakes.

Know that your seemingly unimportant gestures throughout the day could be just what someone else needs at that moment. All of your kind actions add up to a meaningful life. Having the well-being of others in mind is where you start. You move throughout the day knowing you are here for a reason. You can make a difference.

And yes, there's more. There are big things you can do. You can bring more peace, opportunity, and happiness to the world through your work. You can volunteer for causes you believe in. You can create a career that embodies the Second Promise (Do What You Love) and Third Promise (Make a Difference). You can lead a charitable organization. You can join the board of a nonprofit. You can work for a company with a mission that improves the quality of life for people.

There is no single path or roadmap that can direct your every step, and there is no one who has all the answers you seek. The actions you take to fulfill the Third Promise—Make a Difference—will help you find the path to contribute to the world in your own unique way.

Now is the time to give—in a small or a big way—it doesn't matter.

Just start today.

The Good Packer

IF YOU OPEN THE TRUNK OF YOUR CAR AND HAND ME YOUR LUGGAGE—AND I mean all of your luggage—I'll find a way to fit it all in.

No car, no minivan, no SUV scares me. I can fit your stuff in no matter what you drive. You can call my trunk packing a sort of strength; I can do it consistently well, and I enjoy doing it. I've volunteered to pack the family car hundreds of times, and I've been called in for the most difficult of jobs. I'm the go-to guy of trunk packing.

Now, of course, there's a beginning to all success stories. So let me tell you mine.

When I was growing up, my dad, Big Lou, was responsible for packing the family car before all of our vacations. He would bring the bags out of the house and stage them by the car. Then, one by one, he'd find space in the trunk for each bag.

Except one day. Big Lou was having trouble finding a place for the last bag. And so he stepped back to take a better look, and he did the typical big man thing: He crossed his arms, and he started staring down the trunk.

Now, I looked up at Big Lou, and I saw that he was staring. I looked at the bags, and I saw that they weren't moving. So I stepped forward and leaned into the trunk.

I moved a bag to the right.

I moved a bag to the left.

I slipped one back.

I reached down, and I grabbed that last bag.

And, wow! Wouldn't you know it, the bag slipped right into place?! I couldn't believe it. I felt as if I had just laid down the final piece of a jigsaw puzzle.

I looked up at Big Lou. Big Lou looked down at me, and he said, "David, you're a good packer!"

I was nine years old when he told me that, and I was so proud. I was so proud that here I am, at age forty-nine, and I'm still talking about it.

Psychologists have found that when you call out the strengths you see in others, you amplify them. My dad called out my strength nearly four decades ago. But he did more than that. Like a good leader, like a good father, my dad turned that experience into a story, and he told everybody. And he did one more thing. He made sure that I could hear him telling it.

See, when Dad couldn't find space for that last bag, he could have become frustrated and annoyed. He could have become distracted and impatient. He could have missed the opportunity to recognize his son, "the good packer."

But he didn't. He thanked me. He named my strength. And he set in motion a wave of positive energy that continues today.

And that's what fires me up. It's never too late to call out the good packer in someone. If I could ask you to do one thing today, I would ask you to go out and look for the good packer in everyone.

The Bike

A COUPLE OF YEARS AGO I STEPPED OUT OF MY CAR IN A TOYS R US PARKING lot, and I saw a young boy, his mother, and grandmother trying to squeeze a new bicycle into the family car. Well, I stopped and offered to help.

Why?

Because I'm a good packer!

For ten minutes the boy and I tried to get the bike in the car. We moved the bike every which way. We tried everything we could. After we'd been struggling for a while, I heard the mother call the boy's father to say they wouldn't be bringing the bike home. I waved at the mother. I asked for more time.

Why?

Because I'm a good packer.

So, the boy and I tried again. After a few minutes, I stopped. It occurred to me that we might not actually be able to get the bike in the car. I thought I had finally met my match. So, I took a step back.

The little boy must have seen my face because he put up his hand and he said, "Wait." And I waited. The little boy reached into the trunk, grabbed the front tire, moved it just a little bit, and said, "Push." And so I did.

I pushed.

And the bike slipped right into place.

I looked over at the little boy, and he lit up with pride. I smiled, walked over to him, put my hand on his shoulder, and I said, "You're a good packer."

When you recognize people for what they do well—when you focus on bringing out their best—you give them a gift of a lifetime.

Every day you have an opportunity to call out the good packer in someone. Every day you can look for the good in people and make a difference.

That's what the Third Promise is all about.

Third Promise Actions

WHO ARE ALL THE IMPORTANT PEOPLE IN YOUR LIFE PERSONALLY AND professionally? Plan each day this week to make it your Third Promise activity to look for the good in someone and call it out. Recognize them for what they do well.

Butterfly Living

A FEW YEARS AGO, WHEN DAWN AND I WERE IN KEY WEST FOR A LONG weekend, we found ourselves on a street corner, poring over a map with our three- and four-year-old daughters at our side. The map was spread open, and as we went back and forth about what to do next, our girls jumped right in and told us exactly what they wanted to do.

"We want to go to a museum of butterflies," said Ariela and Eliana.

Dawn and I had never been to a museum of butterflies. We looked at the map, and sure enough there it was: a museum of butterflies. How our girls knew about this place, we had no idea. It was near the end of Duvall Street.

Dawn and I looked at each other and said, "Let's go."

When we arrived at the museum, I bought tickets, and we were directed to a special pressurized entrance (you know the kind—the suction is so strong you get a new hairstyle on the way in) at the center of the museum. And as soon as we walked into the main area we were immediately surrounded by thousands and thousands of butterflies, all flapping their multicolored wings. They were absolutely beautiful.

I looked down at our girls. They were jumping up and down and clapping their hands.

I knew we had made the right decision to come to the museum. They were having so much fun.

The Question

I TURNED TO OUR MUSEUM TOUR GUIDE— JUST BECAUSE I WAS CURIOUS —and asked, "How long do butterflies live?"

She said, "About ten days."

I thought to myself, "Ten days. What can you do in ten days?!"

So, I asked her, "What do butterflies do in ten days?!"

The guide stopped, looked at me, and said, "They make the world a more beautiful place."

"Wow," I said. "I never thought about butterflies like that. Thank you."

After we said goodbye, I couldn't stop thinking about what the guide had said. She was right: We all have something to offer the world with the time we have. When we focus our natural gifts on taking care of each other every day, we fulfill the Third Promise.

We Make a Difference

Third Promise Actions

APPRECIATE THE IMPACT YOU HAVE ON YOUR FAMILY, FRIENDS, COWORKERS, and neighbors. Like a butterfly, you have your own way of making the world a little better for everyone. Embrace the opportunity to contribute to others. Your life matters. Make it a point in the coming days to demonstrate the impact you have on others by offering a hand to people in need.

The Law of the Host

DO YOU KNOW THAT FEELING YOU HAVE WHEN YOU ENTER A ROOM AND YOU don't know anyone? You know you're supposed to meet new people, but you don't know where to begin. You feel like a little kid on the playground, hoping someone will invite you to play. I learned that it could be different, at a party in New York City eighteen years ago.

A friend of mine told me to meet him there. He knew the host and said the party would be fun. He gave me the address, and I took a cab to the East Village.

My cab pulled up, I paid the driver, got out, and walked to the front door. It was partially open, and I could see people talking and laughing inside. I opened the door wide and stepped in. No one was there to greet me, so I unbuttoned my coat and scanned the room. I didn't see my friend. I looked at my watch (he must've been running late), and walked in.

I looked around the room. There was no one I knew. The music was loud, people were gathered in small groups, and I felt uncomfortably out of place. Just then a young woman with a warm smile approached me. She was holding a big bag of M&Ms.

She said, "Do you want some?"

"Sure," I said, relieved someone was talking to me.

"Okay, open your hand," she said. The young woman poured some in my hand.

"Thanks." I put one in my mouth, and cradled my hand around the rest.

She said, "Welcome to the party. I'm Susana."

"I'm David. Nice to meet you. Great apartment."

"It's a great place, isn't it?" Susana said.

Then I said, "Thanks for having the party. Everyone seems to be having fun."

She laughed, "The party is great. Lots of cool people. But it's not my party."

"That's funny. I thought it was."

She smiled. "No, the only person I know here is my friend who brought me. She's over there by the kitchen."

"But what about the big bag of M&Ms and the hello?"

She said, "I just wanted to welcome you."

It was then that I understood something I call "The Law of the Host."

Guests and Hosts

WE CAN BE ONE OF TWO PEOPLE IN LIFE. WE CAN BE A GUEST OR A HOST. When we see ourselves as guests, we wait. We wait to be greeted. We wait to be welcomed. We wait to be introduced. Other people have to come to us.

When we see ourselves as hosts, we are the welcomers. We view life as our event. We reach out to others. We smile. We greet people. We help them.

When we play the host, we open ourselves up to new people and experiences, act generously, and give others the opportunity to feel included, appreciated, and loved.

You have a choice—how you show up in life is up to you. Your mindset is what matters. If you feel like a guest, you act like a guest. If you feel like a host, you act like a host.

Playing the good host makes you feel confident and energized, knowing that it is your responsibility, pleasure, and right to interact with everyone. You reach out to people and make sure they are comfortable and feel included.

Ritz Carlton

TO CELEBRATE OUR FIRST WEDDING ANNIVERSARY, DAWN AND I SPLURGED and stayed at a Ritz Carlton in Hawaii. We were living in California at the time, so it struck us as a good opportunity—the perfect occasion—to make the trip.

When we arrived, we were immediately delighted that the staff—each and everyone one of them, at all levels—were so friendly. They were always saying hi with big smiles. One day I was so impressed, I stopped one of the employees, who had just said hello, and thanked him for being so friendly. He said it was his pleasure. I asked him what made everyone so welcoming. He said two things: The hotel hires people who enjoy helping others, and the rule is, if you see a guest within six feet of you, you always say hello. I love that all of the employees of the Ritz Carlton are committed to being hosts.

Our Decision

IT'S EASY TO LIVE LIFE AS A GUEST. ALL YOU HAVE TO DO IS LET PEOPLE COME to you. This approach isn't wrong. It's unobtrusive and can even be respectful, in some instances, but it's conservative, a blending strategy that lets you avoid the risk of standing out.

Stepping out to meet people can lead to disappointment: Not everyone will respond to you the way you would like or expect. But when you see yourself as a host, you shift the focus to other people and make new connections as you welcome them at your church, synagogue, or wherever you worship or gather to be with other people, whether it's a business meeting, conference, club event, or a party.

When you act as a host you are truly alive—and help others come alive, too.

Third Promise Actions

LOOK AT THE VARIOUS ROLES YOU PLAY AT WORK, AT HOME, AND IN YOUR community. Make it a point each day this week to act as a host. Make others feel comfortable, even if that means you'll have to leave your comfort zone to do it. Watch the impact your hosting has on others. You'll be impressed.

Be a "Cycler," Not a "Clicker"

RECENTLY, MY WIFE, DAWN, AND I WERE ASKED TWO QUESTIONS. A FRIEND asked, "Your parents do so much for you; why do you think they are so giving?" We saw the question as a compliment and a tribute to our parents.

A couple weeks later, another friend asked the second question: "You and Dawn do a lot for your parents; how come you do so much for them?" We appreciated this question, too; it recognized what Dawn and I do for our parents. We love our parents, and we want to help make their lives easier and more enjoyable. Until recently, I held these questions separately in my mind; I now see they are part of the same question. Why do we do so much for each other? The answer is that we are in what I call a "Love Cycle."

Love Cyclers

A LOVE CYCLE HAPPENS WHEN PEOPLE IN A RELATIONSHIP DO NOT KNOW who started doing what for whom; they only know that there is constant giving and receiving in the relationship. The love expressed and the good works done on each other's behalf happen so often that there's no purpose in keeping score. People in a Love Cycle are what I call "Love Cyclers."

A friend of mine once had a temporary job counting cars at a busy intersection in New York City. He had to "click his clicker" every time a vehicle of any kind passed by. Although my friend almost lost his mind doing this job, he said he really had to focus so that he could keep clicking.

Clickers

MANY PEOPLE WALK AROUND IN THEIR RELATIONSHIPS WITH THEIR OWN clickers, counting the number of things that other people do for them. They don't want to give more than they get, and they spend valuable time clicking and counting rather than cycling the giving in their relationships. These folks aren't Love Cyclers; they are "Clickers."

Who do you want to be? A Love Cycler or a Clicker?

Here's an easy way to orient your thinking to the Love Cycle: Take the typical marriage vows "to love, honor, and cherish." "Clickers" sit and wait for their spouses to love, honor, and cherish them. "What have you done for me lately?" is the question they ask before they reach out to their spouses. Love Cyclers don't wait—they just go ahead, jump in with both feet—to love, honor, and cherish their spouses.

The University of Washington psychology researcher, John Gottman, discovered that married couples who keep score in their relationships are unhappy. In his book, *The Seven Principles for Making Marriage Work*, Gottman reports, "Happy spouses do not keep tabs on whether their mate is washing dishes as a payback because they cooked dinner. They do it because they generally feel positive about their spouse and their relationship."

Good leaders are Love Cyclers, too. They set the tone at work with their actions. They give, they offer, and they help. They tell stories of people helping them and supporting them. You see them volunteer. On the other hand, Clickers talk about who hasn't helped them, who owes them, and who's giving them a hard time. Clickers are so busy clicking they miss opportunities to give.

When you change your orientation from a Clicker to a Cycler, your life opens wide to opportunities that will continually make a difference.

The bottom line is that Love Cyclers make better spouses, friends, and bosses. Love Cyclers are good for humanity. They don't limit their Cycling to reciprocal relationships. They open their Cycling to the world. They give without expectations of a matching return. They trust in the broader Love Cycle. They fulfill the Third Promise.

When you go to work today and when you go home tonight, think about leaving your clicker behind.

Be a Love Cycler.

Third Promise Actions

MAKE THE FIRST MOVE ALL WEEK, AND HELP OTHERS WITHOUT KEEPING score. Look for at least one opportunity each day to act as a Love Cycler. And if you catch yourself thinking like a Clicker, that's okay—we all do at some point. Just put the clicker down, and Make a Difference in someone's life.

The Power of Your "Love Example"

HAVE YOU EVER THOUGHT ABOUT WHAT YOUR LOVE LOOKS LIKE? IS IT WARM? Is it kind? Is it accepting? Is it passionate? Is it committed? On a family outing many years ago, I learned that the way we show our love makes a powerful difference in the lives of our loved ones.

My parents and I were riding along just outside Augusta, Maine. Dad was driving the car, Mom was next to him in the passenger seat, and I sat behind her in the backseat. We were one of the few cars out that day, as we meandered along the two-lane, tree-lined road on the way to the family cemetery. The sun was shining, and the wind was blowing gently.

Dad pulled over to the side of the road. We stepped out of the car and walked on the gravel between the road and the tall grass. We headed toward the cemetery. Mom, Dad, and I had come to visit the graves of my mother's parents, who were buried in this serene place, nestled among small, family farms.

Mom and Dad walked hand in hand as we approached the family plot. We were the only ones there.

The cemetery was surrounded by an old rock wall, hugged by lilac bushes and framed by maple, pine, and oak trees. For over two centuries the graveyard had been the final home of many of our relatives. As we walked slowly on the recently cut grass, I read the names etched into the tombstones I passed. I wondered how many of these people my grandparents had known. At last, we arrived at the foot of my grandparents resting place.

My grandmother had passed first, so she was buried in the family plot to the left. On her right was her husband, my grandfather, who passed away twelve years later. And between my grandfather's plot and the gravesite of someone we did not know, there was a small patch of grass.

Pointing to it, Mom said, "That was for me."

Dad and I looked down at the ground. There was just enough room for one more plot.

Mom said softly, "My parents wanted to make sure that I was near them if I didn't marry."

Dad and I looked at Mom.

Uncertain, I asked, "Do you want to be buried here?"

Mom hesitated. "There isn't a place for your father," she said. "I wouldn't want to be without him."

I looked at Dad. He was staring straight ahead.

Dad put his arm around Mom, and pulled her into him. He kissed her on the top of her head. "I will always be with you," he said.

He looked at her. "If there's only one plot, it will be for you. They'll just have to lay my ashes around you."

Dad held Mom in his arms. I looked down at the open spot of grass. Mom and Dad reached out to me, and we embraced and held on tight without words.

What We Show

THAT DAY, JUST OFF A COUNTRY ROAD IN MAINE, I SAW TRUE LOVE. I saw how much my parents loved each other—something I'll never forget. And I learned that the love we show is the love we give. "They do not love that do not show their love," wrote Shakespeare. Our loved ones learn through our example.

Every day we have an opportunity to demonstrate our love to the most important people in our lives. Expressing your love in ways people can experience and feel is the single greatest gift you can give another person. Emily Dickinson reminds us, "Unable are the Loved ones to die/ For Love is Immortality."

What is your love example?

Third Promise Actions

THINK OF YOUR PARENTS, SIBLINGS, CHILDREN, SPOUSE, RELATIVES, and friends. How do you show your love? What do you do to make it clear how much you love the people in your life? Don't hold back. Make some of your Third Promise activities focus on demonstrating your love.

Hug Now. Don't Save It.

ONE DAY I ARRIVED HOME FROM THE OFFICE, AND MY DAD WAS STANDING IN the driveway. Dad is six feet two inches tall and wears a full beard. He was talking with two pro-football-sized construction workers. As I approached them, they all turned and looked at me. I said, "Hi Dad. Hey guys." I stepped forward, shook my dad's hand, pulled him into me, hugged him, and gave him a kiss on the cheek. I then walked into the house.

For three generations, my family has done the same thing: We kiss and hug when we see each other. We kiss and hug when we say goodbye. And we don't care who is watching. My parents taught me through their example. My grandmother reinforced this practice by what she said to me thirty-eight years ago. I told this story in *The Law of the Garbage Truck.* I want to share it again with you now.

I was nine years old. It was wintertime in Milwaukee. My family was leaving Northridge Shopping Mall after a movie. Mom, Dad, my brother Mike, and my grandparents were there. And I was mad at my dad. I have no idea why, but I know that I was mad. I was pouting, and I wasn't talking to him.

It was snowing that night, and the temperature was near zero. Dad told us to wait inside the mall so that he could warm up the van and pull it up to the front door.

That's when Nana came up to me and said, "Your father loves you, and you love him. Don't go to bed angry at him. Kiss and hug him before you go to bed tonight. Tell him that you love him. You never know when the Lord will take him from you."

Few words have had such an impact on me as those of my grandmother that night. "You never know when the Lord will take him from you."

Don't Wait

DAWN AND I RECENTLY ATTENDED THE FUNERAL OF A COLLEAGUE'S FATHER who had passed away after a major heart attack. His son was eulogizing him. He said that one minute his father was talking; the next minute he was gone. My colleague was respectful of his father, and he recalled good times. And then he said something that made our hearts sink: "I never did hear my father say he loved me."

My mother taught us to hug, kiss, and say that we love each other when we wake up, when we go to bed, before we leave the house, and before we hang up the phone.

Tony Dungy, famed Super Bowl–winning head football coach, sees it the same way. Dungy lost his eighteen-year-old son, James, a number of years ago. In his eulogy, Coach Dungy said that he had last seen his son at Thanksgiving. They had said goodbye before James left for the airport. Knowing that they would see each other again soon, Dungy didn't think much about the casual way they'd said goodbye. He never did see his son again.

Dungy said, "I never got to hug him again. That's one thing I'll always think about and always remind people to do: Hug 'em every chance you get."

My dad is now eighty-four. He just visited me in my office.

I hugged and kissed him when he arrived.

I hugged and kissed him when he left.

Third Promise Actions

THINK AGAIN ABOUT THE IMPORTANT PEOPLE IN YOUR LIFE. WHAT DO YOU still have to say to the ones you love? What do you still have to do? There's no room for delay—we know too well that life is not guaranteed—put this book down and call, write, or visit someone. Make this your Third Promise activity today. Make it clear how much you care about them and how much they mean to you.

Prefer, Yes. Judge, No.

A FEW YEARS AGO, I NEEDED TO FIX SOMETHING IN THE HOUSE AND NEEDED help fixing it. I called a reputable company that made a good product at a good price and that gave good service. The sales representative I talked to was helpful. When I asked some questions that required his manager's assistance, the representative transferred me to him.

The manager who picked up the phone wasn't very friendly. He wasn't thrilled to answer questions, and his responses were a little curt. That didn't stop me from politely asking every question on my list. In the end, I was happy with his answers, and I ordered the product and service I needed.

Preferences vs. Judgments

IT'S ALWAYS IMPORTANT TO FOCUS ON WHAT MATTERS, AND TO DISTINGUISH between making judgments and having preferences.

I prefer people to be friendly in a business transaction. I see positive human interaction as an opportunity to spread goodwill in the workplace and in the world.

However, not all people who do good work are friendly—but rather than judge them as "not nice people" or "not good guys," focus on their ability to do the job right. You need their help to fix problems; they are not required to be your best friends. Now, if I have two companies to choose from and they're equal by all measures, I will choose the friendlier one. That's my preference.

Having preferences is natural. It's part of being human. Act on them if they're important to you. However, be sparing in your judgments. You can prefer something—and act on that preference—without judging others too harshly.

Third Promise Actions

MAKE A BIG DIFFERENCE EVERY DAY. NOTICE WHEN YOU START JUDGING people. Recognize that what you're really expressing is a preference, and hold back from turning it into a judgment. When you do this, you'll have more energy for what really matters in your life, and you will release people from the weight of your judgments.

Upstream, Downstream:
Where Are You Standing?

MY GRANDFATHER USED TO HIKE ABOUT AN HOUR INTO THE FOREST WITH his fishing rod in one hand and his tackle box and lunch in the other. When he arrived at his special place, he would carefully lay everything down. He would pause for a moment to take in the sights, the smells, and the sounds of his sacred spot. He would thread a worm on the hook of his fishing rod and wade into the stream with his hip boots on.

The stream was about ten feet wide and four feet deep. The stream was pure. It traveled miles through the forest to where he would stand. With it came an abundance of fish.

My grandfather would settle in for hours. There was nothing between him and nature. Nothing between him and God. He was a grateful man. He appreciated what the forest and stream brought to him. He was thankful for the food he could provide his family, and the peace and happiness he felt in the stream.

He was also a responsible man. He knew he was not the only one fishing the stream. As special as his sanctuary was to him, someone downstream was relying on the same beautiful water.

Other People

MY GRANDFATHER KNEW THAT HIS ACTIONS UPSTREAM WOULD IMPACT what happened downstream. He accepted this responsibility, and he honored it. He left no waste and took only the fish he was allowed.

Other fishermen were not so thoughtful. They would stand in the same stream and not consider how their actions affected anyone else's experience. They might take too many fish: "It's a big stream. No one's going to notice."

In our own lives, sometimes we focus only on where we stand in the stream. We're only concerned with what's in front of us. We forget that there is always an upstream and a downstream—that we are affected by those who came before us and that we affect those who come after us. Someone is always impacted by our thoughts, feelings, and actions.

Third Promise Actions

WHAT THOUGHTFUL ACTIONS CAN YOU TAKE THAT WILL POSITIVELY IMPACT others downstream at work, at home, or in your community? And how can you communicate your gratitude to the kind and helpful people upstream?

We thrive in life when we appreciate the good that has come before us and take responsibility for what we pass on to others. Our ability to positively influence others is a privilege and a responsibility.

Don't Get Distracted
by Differences

ABOUT TWENTY YEARS AGO, I WAS WORKING IN MÁLAGA, THE CAPITAL OF the southern region of Andalucía, Spain, as an intern for a real estate development company. One sunny afternoon, as I was standing in line in a small grocery store near my apartment, I learned that the differences among us do not have to divide us.

People were standing in front of me and behind me. We were packed tightly together in a single file line. Everyone was pretty much keeping to themselves, except for saying an occasional, "Hola," or, "Buenos días."

After a short wait, I reached a point where I could see two registers. I was next. There was hardly any space between me and the two people who were checking out. The counters were not large enough for me to unload my groceries, so, I did the only thing I could: I waited for the next available register.

Then I heard someone say in Spanish, "Excuse me. Choose a line."

I turned around, and the man behind me was waving for me to advance.

"Choose a line," he said again.

I looked at him. I looked at the registers. No one had moved; the customers were still checking out.

I looked back at him, and again, he said, "Choose a line."

I smiled and said, "Señor, I'm already in line. There's no room to go anywhere. The registers are busy. I'll move when one is free."

And he said, "No, you have to choose a line."

Forming a Line

NOW, ONE THING I KNOW HOW TO DO IS FORM A LINE. I DIDN'T NEED a tutorial.

So, I said, "Señor, I'll move as soon as a register is free."

I was thinking, "This guy has got a problem." That is, until everyone behind him started nodding and saying to me, "Choose a line."

"I'm not moving," I said to myself. "There's no need for me to get any closer to the customers in front of me. These guys just need to learn how to keep a line." I held my ground. I knew I was right.

Finally, it was my turn. The cashier bagged my groceries, and I paid. I left the store and headed down the street with bags in both hands. I was still thinking about what happened: How could they all agree that I was lining up wrong?

Suddenly I stopped. I looked up and saw that all the street signs were in Spanish. The music playing around me was in Spanish. The conversations of the people walking past me were in Spanish. That's when I got it. I started laughing. I said to myself, "I'm in Spain. If this is how they line up in Spain, I'll do it their way. I'll squeeze in. I'll hover. I don't have to teach everyone the way I do it."

Understanding Differences

AS IT TURNED OUT, I LEARNED THAT SPANIARDS IN MÁLAGA (MALAGEÑOS) have much looser rules about lining up than I was accustomed to. Sometimes just crowding around a cashier is acceptable. And you know something? Somehow, people still get the help they need.

So often, we are distracted by what we perceive as differences between how we do business—the differences between us and other people's customs and culture. What seems odd to us bothers us. "That's not the way it should be done," we think. And then we get upset. We get stuck on being right instead of looking after more important things. We do this in our marriages, in our careers, and in our communities. Thankfully, we can change this in an instant.

In an increasingly interconnected world, the more we know and respect about each other's customs and cultures the better our ability to work and live productively and harmoniously together.

In 1999, I took my wife, Dawn, to Spain on our honeymoon. We had a wonderful time. And we even lined up in Málaga . . . their way.

Third Promise Actions

THINK OF A PRACTICE OR CUSTOM YOU DO NOT UNDERSTAND. FIND OUT why it exists and why it matters. Then, make it a point to change your perspective and appreciate that there are alternative ways of doing things in this world. When you do, you fulfill the Third Promise.

Be grateful for differences.

It makes the world interesting.

Who Do You Run To?

THE RECORD FOR THE FIFTY-YARD DASH AT LAKE BLUFF ELEMENTARY SCHOOL in Shorewood, Wisconsin, was set in the mid-1950s. One spring morning in 1976, I was determined to break it. I was a fifth grader who had raced his friends many times, but I had never raced for our school record with an official stop watch. My classmates and I were all gathered by the starting line on our old asphalt playground. I was excited, and I was nervous. My friends were betting I could do it.

I walked past my classmates and stepped up to the starting line. I looked at my gym teacher, Mr. Buddy Wolf. He blew his whistle, and I took off running. I pumped my legs and arms as fast as I could. Six-point-five seconds later, I leaned into the finish line, and I heard the click of Mr. Wolf's stop watch. I turned around just as fast as I could to hear Mr. Wolf say, "You just broke the school record!"

My class burst into applause! I jogged back to everyone. My buddies slapped me on the back and punched me in the arm. I was in fifth-grade heaven. And then my thoughts turned to lunchtime. I wanted to get home to tell Mom and call Dad at work.

One period later, the lunch bell rang. I sprinted out of the classroom, down the stairs, out the side door, and ran six blocks home. I opened the back door of the house, turned into the kitchen, and saw Mom making a grilled cheese sandwich and a bowl of tomato soup. I kissed Mom, and then I told her all about the race, the record, and my classmates cheering.

She asked me to tell the whole story from start to finish, with every detail included. So, I reenacted everything. She clapped and she hugged me. And then I called Dad and relived the whole experience. He was thrilled for me. It was one of the best days of my life.

Good News

WHO DO YOU RUN TO? WHO HELPS YOU CELEBRATE YOUR ACHIEVEMENTS? And why do you run to these special people? Why are they the first on your list? What is it about these individuals that attracts you to them?

The psychologist Shelly Gable, and her fellow researcher Harry Reis, discovered that there are four principal ways people respond to the good news of others, and only one of them makes a positive difference in a relationship:

1. Active and Constructive: They're "enthusiastic;" they're "almost more happy and excited than I am;" and "they ask lots of questions."

2. Passive and Constructive: They try "not to make a big deal out of it, but are happy for me," or they "say little, but I know they are happy for me."

3. Active and Destructive: They "often find a problem with it," or they "point out the potential downsides of the good event."

4. Passive and Destructive: They "seem disinterested;" they don't care much; or they don't "pay much attention to me."

Gable and Reis's research showed that the people who have a measurably positive impact on your enthusiasm, joy, and happiness in life are the ones who respond actively and constructively to your good news. They also discovered that people who receive active and constructive feedback in close personal relationships report higher relationship well-being, as indicated by measures of intimacy and marital satisfaction.

Sharing

NOW, NOT EVERYONE IS AS SENSITIVE OR IN TUNE WITH OTHERS AS YOU might wish. It is what it is. It's not bad or good. So sometimes you have to telegraph your good news. You need to let people know with your words and emotions that you're excited. You can simply start by saying, "I'm excited about something. Can I share it with you?"

Two things will happen when you do this: First, you're communicating to the people you care about that you have good news to share with them; and second, your question gives them a moment to redirect their attention from whatever it was they were doing before you approached them with your good news. You also increase the likelihood that you'll receive an active and constructive response. If you don't telegraph your excitement, you may overwhelm them by jumping into an update without warning.

Third Promise Actions

THINK ABOUT THE PEOPLE YOU LOVE AND CARE ABOUT. DO YOUR CHILDREN run to you with good news? Does your spouse? Do your friends? Do your coworkers?

Think of the opportunities you have to help bring out the best in the people you care about. Think about the joy you can amplify in their lives when you respond actively and constructively to their good news. And, like my mom and dad did for me, think about the lasting memories you are helping to create for the people you love.

Make a Difference.

Welcome people to run to you with their good news.

Give Up the
Game Show Mindset

WHEN I WAS A SENIOR IN HIGH SCHOOL, I HAD A CLASSMATE WHO WANTED to answer every question the teacher asked. After about five questions, no one could miss the fact that there was a student in the back row waving his hand wildly, bouncing out of his seat, and doing everything else he could think of to get the teacher's attention.

This student was a smart guy and a good guy, but he simply wasn't aware that he was crowding out other people's contributions. He was so concerned with grabbing every opportunity to provide an answer that he took his eyes off his relationship with others. He had what I call a "Game Show Mindset."

The Mindset

IF YOU HAVE THE GAME SHOW MINDSET, YOU LOVE BEING RIGHT ALL THE time and jump on every opportunity to show what you know. I call people who have this mindset, and who travel around with a huge invisible answer button that they're ready to press at any time, "Game Show Contestants."

This Game Show behavior happens at home, too. I should know—I've been caught with my hand on the answer button, too.

My wife Dawn had rearranged a few rooms in our home one weekend while I was out of town leading a workshop in New York City. Dawn did a beautiful job in the house and worked very hard; I was impressed, and she was rightly proud of herself. The day after I returned from my trip she started to apply her talent to the upstairs office. And then I started playing the role of the Game Show Contestant.

I said things like, "That won't fit, I already measured it," and "That doesn't look good if it's not centered." And then I carried my big answer button to the kitchen and started in again, "That snack is not as healthy as you think, and so on." Like my high school friend I was so caught up in "being right," I missed the chance to be supportive, appreciative, and encouraging.

Don't Miss the Bids

RELATIONSHIP RESEARCHER JOHN GOTTMAN WOULD SAY THAT I WAS SO focused on having the right answer that I missed what he calls "bids." In his book *The Relationship Cure,* he says, "A bid can be a question, a gesture, a look, a touch—any single expression that says, 'I want to feel connected to you.'" Gottman's research shows that most relationships succeed because of the many small interactions people have. He says, "By becoming aware and mindful of such moments, we can give and receive the intimacy and support we all need from our closest relationships."

Let's take Gottman's advice and pay attention to our relationships. We can take our hands off the answer button; there's no need for us to jump out of our seats to answer every question.

Third Promise Actions

GIVE OTHERS A CHANCE TO CONTRIBUTE AS OFTEN AS POSSIBLE, AND allow them to shine. It will make a big difference in their lives. Forget about racking up points for being "right" on the imaginary scoreboard: The rewards will be much greater.

Identify how you can create more opportunities for others, and then step back so that they can step forward. The light that shines on them will illuminate your life.

Lessons from an Unexpected Letter

A COUPLE YEARS AGO, I RECEIVED AN UNEXPECTED LETTER FROM A FRIEND that taught me some very important lessons. I value them so much that I asked my friend for his permission to share the letter with you. I have three reasons for wanting you to know the backstory of these lessons, but first, here's the letter:

David,

It was almost five years ago that I first decided to look you up. Allow me to explain the reason behind my decision to contact you after so many years. It will explain how I think you have been helping people for a long time.

I have been a police officer in Milwaukee for almost fifteen years. I was very good at it, and I felt that I was benefiting society. However, it was an extremely stressful occupation for me because, in spite of my successes, for many of those years I had virtually no skills for managing stress and its effects on my health.

Picture this scene: An almost middle-aged, overweight, out of shape, half-asleep cop with a bad attitude is hauling his aching frame from a squad car at 3:00 a.m. into a convenience store for his sugar and caffeine fix to get him through the rest of the shift. A 20 oz. Mountain Dew was the usual fuel of choice for this purpose.

For some reason unbeknownst to me, I grabbed chocolate milk that night instead and was instantly reminded of a young David Pollay spooning sugar into a bowl as he explained how much of it we consume in a typical day. Do you remember your speech: "Sugar: The Hidden Menace"? I remember you said there were six to eight teaspoonfuls of sugar in each carton of chocolate milk (Pollay, 1978ish).

That incident five years ago in the convenience store was a turning point in my life. It was then that a confluence of three ideas hit me all at once. First, I needed to gain control over my health, which was in a sorry state of affairs. By simply heeding the advice of your speech I was able to return to my normal weight. After much struggle, I kicked the soda habit and in so doing I lost the aches and pains.

Second, after ten years on the streets, I realized I needed a different job with a little less stress. I then requested and received a transfer to the Identification Division of the Milwaukee PD. There I was trained as a CSI photographer. Third, I decided to return to college. I am now in my third year working toward a bachelor's degree in communication.

My kids are also benefiting from your speech because I have a good mental image of how much sugar they are eating on a daily basis. Jakob, 5, and Louis, 3, are my two wonderful boys who are also responsible for motivating me to get off my butt and continue to make the important changes in my life.

David, all of this was sparked by a flashback to your speech. It was ahead of its time and delivered in a way that was impossible to forget. I just stored it away and dug it up at a most opportune time.

Thank you, David.

Andrew Smith

Impact

HERE ARE THE THREE REASONS FOR TELLING ANDREW'S STORY.

First, his letter was a gift to me. How often do people from your distant past look you up to tell you that you made a difference in their lives? Who are the people in your life to whom you can give a similar gift?

Second, Andrew's story is inspiring. His life reminds us that we are never stuck on a path without options: We always have a choice. Andrew took the best of his life—his meaningful roles as a guardian of his community and a father of two boys—and improved it by increasing his health, furthering his education, and pursuing his mission of inspiring others to achieve their dreams in life.

Third, Andrew's letter taught me that we do not always know the impact we are having on others. Who knew that a speech that I gave when I was thirteen years old would make a difference in Andrew's life nearly thirty years later. It is heartening to think that our roles as parents, friends, and colleagues may have a positive influence on others. We are reminded to give our best to what we care about most: our family, our friends, our work, our education, our community. It is completely possible, as I learned from Andrew, that the results of our efforts can have a long-lasting, positive influence on others.

Andrew fulfilled the Third Promise: He made the effort to thank me for the impact I've had on his life. Now it's my turn. Thank you Andrew for the impact your letter has had on mine.

Third Promise Actions

WHAT WORK ARE YOU DOING THAT COULD HAVE A LONG-LASTING IMPACT on others? Embrace the importance of your efforts, and recognize the impact your work could have for years to come.

Thank You, Ms. Zwitter

"SHOREWOOD HIGH SCHOOL, MAY I HELP YOU?"

"Yes, Hi. My name is David Pollay, class of 1983. I was hoping to speak with Ms. Zwitter. She was my ninth-grade algebra teacher."

"Oh, I'm sorry, Ms. Zwitter retired last year," said the school administrator.

I had a sinking feeling that I had waited too long to call.

"Is there a way I could call her? Do you have her number?" I asked.

"I wish I could, but school district policy won't allow me to share it with you."

"I understand."

"But if you give me your name again and a telephone number, I can call her and let her know you called. I don't know if she'll return the call, but I can pass along the message."

"Thank you. That would be great."

Class

THIRTY YEARS AGO I SAT IN THE SECOND ROW, SECOND SEAT FROM THE right in Ms. Zwitter's class. She was a demanding teacher. She expected everyone to work hard. She expected everyone to do well. She expected nothing less from me. The problem, in her eyes, was that I received a B for my first-semester grade. That wasn't good enough for her. She thought I wasn't trying hard enough. So, Ms. Zwitter pulled me aside and told me how I could up my game and earn an A in the second semester. I took her advice. I studied, asked questions, and paid more attention in class. I could do it.

Ms. Zwitter reminded me that I was a good football player and that the better grades I got, the more opportunities I would have to play in college. I would even have better schools from which to choose.

Connecting

I HUNG UP THE PHONE FEELING AS IF I HAD MISSED MY OPPORTUNITY TO reach her. It had been thirty years. Thousands of students had come before and after me.

I stepped away from my desk, and I started walking out of the office. The phone rang. I turned around and answered it on the second ring.

"Pollay, what are you doing!" she said. I could hear the smile in her voice.

"Ms. Zwitter!" I said.

"What are you calling me for?! The school office just said you called."

"Ms. Zwitter, I wanted to thank you for everything you did for me freshman year."

"What?"

"Yeah, you challenged me. You expected more of me. You didn't leave me alone. You prodded me. You encouraged me. You believed in me."

"We had fun, didn't we?" she said.

"We sure did," I said.

"David, it's so nice of you to call me after all these years. I've had many students, but not many have come back to say thanks. I tried hard to be a good teacher. I'm so glad I made a difference."

I told her I would put our conversation in a letter. I wanted her to have my gratitude on paper.

We talked for a few more minutes. She said she had retired after thirty-six years of teaching. She told me about all the teachers I knew who had retired, and she told me about the few who were still teaching. We shared some more memories, had a few good laughs, and said we would stay in touch.

A Phenomenon

THERE IS A PHENOMENON YOU'LL EXPERIENCE WHEN YOU EXPRESS gratitude to others. You'll notice that when you sincerely thank someone, it will have a First Promise effect on you: You'll feel joy. Doing good leads to feeling good—that's the beauty of gratitude. I call this the "boomerang effect": When you send out gratitude, it comes right back to you.

In his book, *A Primer in Positive Psychology*, the University of Michigan psychologist Christopher Peterson wrote, "In our experience with many dozens of gratitude letters . . . they 'work' 100 percent of the time in the sense that the recipient is moved, often to tears, and the sender is gratified as well."

We get nowhere in life without help. Every step of our lives someone is helping us. And we rarely take the time to go back and meaningfully thank the people who have made the biggest difference in our lives. When we thank people, we fulfill the Third Promise. Andrew thanked me. I thanked Ms. Zwitter. Who are you going to thank?

Third Promise Actions

MAKE A LIST OF PEOPLE YOU WANT TO THANK, AND PLAN TO SEND YOUR letters and make your calls over the next few weeks and months. You're going to make a lot of people happy.

Giving Beyond Self-interest

MIKE MALLOY, A JUNIOR AT SHOREWOOD HIGH SCHOOL IN SHOREWOOD, Wisconsin, was the star linebacker on our football team in 1984. I was one of two sophomores who made the varsity team that year, and I was the starting running back. During the first game of the season, I scored the winning touchdown, and I was also injured. I had taken a hit directly to my elbow from the helmet of the other team's all-conference linebacker. Although I was able to play the rest of the game, the next day I could not bend my arm and had to sit out the next game.

The following week, I was well enough to return to playing, but the coach only put me in during the fourth quarter. I thought the reason I had been left on the sidelines was because of my injury. I was wrong. There was another reason. Before I tell you what that was, let me set the stage.

When I had to sit out the second game of the season because of my elbow injury, Mike took my place. We won the game, and he was the star. He ran for more than 100 yards (a mark of a great game as a running back) and scored two touchdowns. The next week, my doctors told me I would be ready to play on Friday, since my recovery was nearly complete. But my coaches told me that Mike was going to start again as running back. I would be watching the game from the sidelines.

The Reason

THE FOLLOWING MONDAY, I WAS SITTING NEXT TO MIKE IN SPANISH CLASS. We had a few minutes before the bell rang, signaling the start of class. Mike leaned over to me. He said, "Dave, do you know the reason you sat for most of last Friday's game?"

"Coach was being careful as I was coming off an injury," I said.

"Dave, that's not it," Mike said. "Coach had another reason."

I didn't say anything. I had no idea why the coach would keep me from playing if I was healthy.

Mike continued, "The reason coach benched you was because you arrive late to our warm-up drills almost every day."

"But I don't do it on purpose. You know I get my ankles taped," I answered defensively.

"What I'm telling you is that you're not going to get your starting position back if you keep coming late to practice. You've got to get on the field in time for our drills."

Then it hit me. My replacement at running back was telling me what I needed to do to take back my position—to take it away from him. "Thanks, Mike," I said. "I appreciate the heads-up."

That afternoon, I got ready as fast as I have ever suited up. I arrived on the practice field before we assembled for warm-ups. I was not late again.

The Result

MIKE GAVE ME A GIFT OFF THE FIELD. HE HELPED ME GET MY POSITION back. He also showed me what true leadership is: He gave beyond his self-interest. He did the right thing for the team, for the "organization."

Mike also gave me a gift on the field. During the rest of my sophomore season and during my junior year, he was my fullback, blocking for me on nearly every play. Our team went on to win the conference championship my junior year, and I scored the winning touchdown. For the first time in years, our town's high school football team played in the state championship quarterfinals. Both of us were selected to the all-conference and all-area football teams after the season. Mike was the captain of our team that year, and I followed him as captain my senior year.

Like the story of Luz Long and Jesse Owens, Mike chose sportsmanship over self-interest. He made a difference in my life, and I'll forever be grateful.

Third Promise Actions

THINK OF ALL THE PEOPLE YOU KNOW PERSONALLY AND PROFESSIONALLY. Consider what input you could provide them that would help change their lives. Mike saw beyond his short-term success as my replacement. He wanted to be a part of the best Shorewood team ever, and he knew the role I could play in that success. Think of the Mike Malloys in your life, and thank them. And then look out for the next opportunity to be a Mike Malloy yourself.

Making a Difference
No Matter the Circumstances

I USED TO DO IT EVERY TIME I WENT TO AN ART MUSEUM. I WOULD VIEW A painting that I liked, and then I would head for the wall directly to the right of it. I was careful not to disturb anyone's view on my approach, so I would make a big swing to the right and then inch up the wall until I reached the little metal plaque next to the painting.

I was looking for something in particular.

Yes, I was interested in the name of the painting, who painted it, and the year in which it was completed. But I mostly wanted to know one thing. I wanted to know how long the artist had lived. I was always relieved and happy when I saw that the artist had lived a long life, and I was disappointed when I saw that it had been a short one. For as long as I can remember, I thought a good life was a long life.

David Saltzman taught me another lesson.

I met David during a Yale summer program in London in 1987. We were enrolled at the Paul Mellon Centre for British Art. We were there to study art, architecture, and literature. Although I was two years ahead of him in school, we struck up a friendship.

In addition to being a brilliant student, David was a talented writer and artist. He wrote and drew a weekly comic strip for the *Yale Herald*, and he drew weekly editorial cartoons for the *Yale Daily News*. David was also a good guy. But what was to come would show his real character.

Rising Above

DAVID WAS DIAGNOSED WITH HODGKIN'S DISEASE HIS SENIOR YEAR. Following the news, he immediately went into treatment. He did everything he was supposed to do, but he would not leave school. He found the strength to complete his studies. He graduated on time with the rest of his class and received the David Everett Chantler Award as "the senior who throughout his college career best exemplified the qualities of courage and strength of character and high moral purpose." David did something more. He determined he would finish a book he was writing and illustrating, *The Jester Has Lost His Jingle*. He wanted to share a message of hope with children and their parents, however difficult their circumstances.

David said it this way in his journal, "The best we can do is live life, enjoy it and know it is meant to be enjoyed—know how important and special every time . . . moment . . . person is."

David finished his book, and there are nearly 400,000 books in circulation. *The Jester Has Lost His Jingle* received critical acclaim, garnering the praise of famed authors, Maurice Sendak (*Where The Wild Things Are*), Charles Schulz (*Peanuts*), and Gary Trudeau (*Doonesbury*).

Legacy

DAVID DID NOT LET HIS DISEASE STOP HIM FROM MAKING A DIFFERENCE. IN fact, it inspired him to help others even more. I'm one of the many people who has benefited from his message. I bought multiple copies for my family and friends. My daughters have practically memorized parts of the book.

David's book has had a positive impact on so many people. His message has comforted families facing illness and death, and it has helped children increase their love of reading.

I learned from David that it's not how long we live but the difference we make with the years we have.

David died eleven days before his twenty-third birthday. His life was short, but what he gave us is everlasting.

Thank you, David.

Third Promise Actions

THE TIME TO ACT IS NOW. WHEN I MET DAVID IN LONDON, WE HAD NO IDEA what was awaiting him. None of us knows what lies ahead.

Think about the things that may be blocking you from giving as much as you can. What is limiting your contribution? Take it on, and determine to get past it. Be inspired by David, think big, and give at the highest level you are capable of giving.

Giving Beyond Loss

BARBARA SALTZMAN, DAVID'S MOTHER, HAD BEEN AT HIS SIDE DURING HIS hospital stay. To be with David, Barbara had taken several leaves of absence from her job as editor of the *Los Angeles Times*'s daily Entertainment section. She wanted her son to always be surrounded by love, and she wanted to be his greatest advocate in the hospital. Before his death, David had received every available treatment, including a bone marrow transplant, but despite all the efforts to save him, and the outpouring of love from his family and friends, David passed away on March 2, 1990.

Barbara was devastated. She had always thought he would pull through. No mother—or father—should have to face the death of a child. There is no greater loss. Along with her husband, Joe, and their older son Michael, Barbara mourned the loss of her son. David left a great hole in the lives of his family and friends that is still felt today.

The Book

DAVID WAS GONE, BUT HIS DREAM COULD BE KEPT ALIVE. BARBARA WAS determined to do whatever was needed to get *The Jester Has Lost His Jingle* published and to make sure that it was printed in the best way to bring out the brilliant colors of David's drawings and the story's creative rhymes.

Barbara signed with one of the best literary agents, but despite her efforts, publishers weren't interested in bringing out the book in a way that would fully illustrate the beauty of David's artwork and writing. They said the book would have to be a paperback, printed in black and white, and the text would have to be cut from sixty-four to thirty-two pages. They even said that his rhymes would have to be converted into prose since rhyme "wasn't selling." That was enough for Barbara and Joe: They decided to publish the book themselves. They mortgaged their house to finance the cost of production and paid attention to every detail; they wanted the book to reflect David's vision. Five years after David's death, *The Jester Has Lost His Jingle* was on bookstore shelves with an afterward by Maurice Sendak. Barbara fulfilled her promise: She brought her son's message of hope into the world, a message that she relied on herself to keep on living.

The Mission

BARBARA HAD MORE TO DO. NATIONWIDE RESPONSE TO THE BOOK from families, educators, librarians, and medical professionals encouraged the Saltzmans to create The Jester & Pharley Phund (named after the characters in the book) a nonprofit organization (www.thejester.org) dedicated to helping ill children, especially those with cancer. Barbara wanted to give these children and their parents the hope and laughter they would need and deserve to carry them through the worst times in life. The Jester & Pharley Phund also runs literacy programs aimed at boosting character development and igniting a love for reading.

David's book has now been given to thousands of children in hospitals, shelters, foster care programs, underserved schools, and other special needs facilities. When children are scared or worried, Barbara wants the Jester to be there in support. She has dedicated much of her life to carrying out her son's message. When I asked Barbara about her mission and David's message, she said: "I want children to know that they have the power to determine their own lives, that they can turn sadness upside down, and that they're empowered to move forward. Children need to know that they have potential and their lives have meaning, and that they can make things better not only for themselves, but for other people. And sometimes it's just the simplest thing, such as sharing a smile or a laugh. Children can control their feelings and make their lives better, even when everything seems to be going wrong. It's also important for children to care about others, and to help them. Those are the two key messages of the book and our programs."

Continued Impact

LAST YEAR, AT THE WRAP-UP CELEBRATION OF A READING PROGRAM I
lead at Village Academy in Delray Beach, Florida, I read *The Jester Has
Lost His Jingle* to the first grade. The kids loved the book, acting it out with
me as we went along. And then, as a surprise gift, we presented each first
grader with a copy of the book. We wanted the children to have their own
copy to take home and share with their families. Barbara and two of her
nonprofit's loyal funders, Maria Restrepo Forte and John M. Forte, made
the donation possible.

We do not know how long we will live or how long our loved ones will live.
We have only the opportunity to make a difference with the years we have.
David Saltzman blessed us with his life. And Barbara Saltzman is ensuring that
David's contribution continues to help people around the world.

Thank you, Barbara.

Third Promise Actions

TRAGEDY HAS A DEVASTATING IMPACT ON ALL OF US. THE QUESTION WE
must ask ourselves is, how long will we live in devastation? Is there a
point when we can turn some of our attention and energy away from our
heartache to a worthy cause?

Barbara told me that you never get over the loss of a child; the hurt
is always there. But life is more than just your pain; it's an opportunity to
ease the burden of others through your giving. It's an opportunity to find
joy again. When you're ready, follow Barbara's example, and let your giving
carry you beyond your loss.

Giving Quietly

IN 1966, MY GRANDFATHER—BUMPA POLLAY—WAS IN NEW YORK CITY ON business. While he was there, he visited my parents and me in our apartment on West 24th Street in Chelsea. I was nine months old. After Bumpa and my parents finished dinner, they put me in a stroller and took what they thought would be a leisurely walk around the neighborhood.

While they were walking, my mother began to feel pain in her stomach. The pain grew progressively worse, and everyone quickly returned to the apartment. By midnight, Mom was vomiting. The pain was so intense, all she could do was lay down on the bathroom floor. She describes the pain as worse than natural childbirth.

After a trip to the local hospital emergency room, she was sent home with a placebo (the doctors on call were convinced that Mom was suffering from a menstrual issue that would soon pass). But the pain didn't pass; it got worse. After calling all afternoon (it was a Saturday), my father finally reached Mom's doctor. Dad told him that the pill the doctors at the hospital had given Mom wasn't working. Mom's doctor immediately ordered her to go to the hospital.

Upon arrival, Mom says she was hooked up to every machine imaginable. The doctors quickly diagnosed her pain to be due to acute pancreatitis. She was immediately put on a treatment regimen. Mom's doctor said that had she gone on much longer without treatment she would have died.

Two weeks into her hospital stay, Mom's gallbladder was removed. During surgery, the doctors discovered she had twenty-seven seed gallstones—one of which had escaped and was wreaking havoc in her system by creating a toxic blockage. The doctors made an incision that started below her belly button and ended above her solar plexus. Mom's stay in the hospital lasted four weeks.

Bumpa's Visit

COMPOUNDING MY MOTHER'S CRITICAL HEALTH ISSUE WAS THE WEIGHTY problem of how everything would be paid. Dad had recently started a new job, but his insurance had not kicked in. My parents would have to pay out of pocket. The cost would be great, eventually totaling more than $4,000 (nearly $29,000 in today's dollars). At that time, it was not possible for my parents to pay that sum.

The day after Mom was admitted to the hospital, a major snowstorm hit New York City. The city shut down. Cars were buried in snow. The plows were not moving. Businesses were closed, and people were staying indoors; but my grandfather was not one of them. He was trudging through the snow to get to the hospital to check on Mom, and he wanted to talk to my dad.

When he arrived at the hospital, my dad gave him an update on what was happening with Mom—her stay in the hospital would be long. Bumpa knew about Dad's job and that he had no insurance. When it was time to leave, Bumpa looked at Dad and told him what he had come to say: He would pay for Mom's medical care. He then made his way through the snow back to his hotel.

One month later, Bumpa quietly paid the hospital bill. Mom and Dad thanked him profusely, and Bumpa said it was what he wanted to do. And that was that. He never mentioned his gift again.

My grandfather was a modest man. He was not one to draw attention to himself; he believed that one should give meaningfully and quietly, and to do what you know is right. He knew that getting recognition is not the goal. Helping others is the goal, and that's enough.

Third Promise Actions

WHEN YOU GIVE BECAUSE YOU BELIEVE IT'S THE RIGHT THING TO DO—
whatever the recognition you may or may not receive—you unleash the
full power of the Third Promise. In giving, be guided by your heart. You
will know what's right.

PART 4

The 3 Promises Challenge

"Your time is limited, so don't waste it living someone else's life. Don't be trapped by dogma—which is living with the results of other people's thinking. Don't let the noise of other's opinions drown out your own inner voice. And most importantly, have the courage to follow your heart and intuition. They somehow already know what you truly want to become. Everything else is secondary."

—Steve Jobs

WHAT WE ORGANIZE OUR LIVES AROUND DETERMINES OUR EXPERIENCES and our possibilities.

How we focus our energy, resources, and attention is within our control. We have the freedom to make, honor, and fulfill the 3 Promises in our personal, as well as professional, relationships.

The beauty of the 3 Promises is that they are available to everyone, regardless of age, education, skills, knowledge, experience, religion, race, ethnicity, culture, or nationality. The 3 Promises serve everyone equally. As soon as you make the 3 Promises, their power is activated. Their potential is released when you consciously choose the actions that support them.

No matter what your circumstances may be, there is always an opening to live the 3 Promises. The opening may be small, but it exists. And when you fill that possibility with all the joy you are able to muster, with passion for something that you love to do, and with determination to make a difference in someone else's life, you greatly expand that opening to live a brighter and more beautiful life.

It's time to go one step further to integrate the 3 Promises into a daily plan. It's time for you to have additional proof that the 3 Promises can transform your life.

The 3 Promises 3-Day Challenge

THE PLAN IS SIMPLE. FOR THREE DAYS MAKE AND FULFILL YOUR 3 PROMISES. All you have to do is choose actions from the preceding chapters to support each promise. That's it.

Here's why it's so important to follow the plan: You're after three wins each day: A win of joy, a win of passion in your work, and a win of giving to someone else. At times they'll be big wins, and sometimes they'll be small wins. The bottom line: All wins are valuable.

The *New York Times* investigative reporter, Charles Duhigg, writes in his book, *The Power of Habit*: "A huge body of research has shown that small wins have enormous power, an influence disproportionate to the accomplishments of the victories themselves . . . . Small wins fuel transformative changes by leveraging tiny advantages into patterns that convince people that bigger achievements are within reach."

Planner, Gatherer, Hunter

IF YOU'RE A PLANNER, YOU'LL IDENTIFY THE ACTIVITIES YOU WANT TO PURSUE the night before or first thing in the morning. You'll schedule them, put them in your planner or journal, and look forward to them. You'll do them, and you'll congratulate yourself for accomplishing them.

Brenda Richterkessing, an associate broker with Keller Williams Realty and an accomplished professional photographer and artist, said this about her experience with the 3 Promises Challenge: "I learned that I really need to plan and commit to each promise if I am to really accomplish them each day. When I write them down it is more likely to happen. For example, in accomplishing the Third Promise, Make a Difference, I met with a friend who is going into the financial planning industry. At his request, I gave him the names of three people I know that he might talk to as he works to build his clientele."

Richterkessing continued, "He followed up with me, requesting their contact info. I kept putting off this task! Finally, as I reflected on accomplishing the Third Promise, Make a Difference, I wrote down my commitment to him as a valued friend. Once I wrote it down as a commitment, I completed the task! I sent a personal email introducing him to each referral. It felt great and set my day off in a positive direction. He appreciated the gesture, and to my surprise, I even received emails from those I referred thanking me for connecting them to him."

On the other hand, you may be more of a gatherer. As joyful opportunities, possibilities to express your passions, and invitations to contribute arise, you take them in. You accept them openly as they come. You feel the contentment of having recognized opportunities and having pursued them.

The award-winning middle school teacher, Ron Wilber, shared an experience he had recently. An opportunity to give presented itself to Ron, and he embraced it. "While on my golf cart this evening, we saw a young teen get off the activity bus. I offered to give him a lift, and he accepted. The lift ended up being a mile and a half in distance. Carrying that heavy backpack after a hard workout at school would have taken him forty-five minutes. It was such a blessing to make a small difference in his life, even if it was just for a short time."

Then again, you may be a hunter. You see life as a chance to create opportunities in situations that occur throughout the day. You're different from the planner because you don't always schedule what you're going to accomplish each day. And you're different from the gatherer because you're more proactive about creating possibilities as you go.

Randy Salim, painter, teacher, and poet, reflected on his approach to fulfilling the 3 Promises: "I can see the increased awareness of what I am going to do today and filling in the buckets as I go: just cleaned up the house . . . that makes Amanda happy (bucket #3), sending an email to my friend (bucket #3), drinking a hot cup of tea (bucket #1), going to pick up Leela and do some art with her (bucket #1, 2), going to write some before I get her (bucket #1, 2), and then edit Thara's essay (bucket #3)."

While some of us fit these profiles pretty well, many of us are hybrids. I like to start with a plan, but I love it when an opportunity arises to fulfill a promise. Other days I like going into each situation with a filter that helps me identify an opportunity to experience joy, use my gifts, or help someone.

The Fulfillment of Others

CONSIDER THE POWERFUL IMPACT THE 3 PROMISES WILL HAVE ON your relationships.

> *Your children will blossom when you commit to enjoying each day, developing and using your gifts, and making a difference in the world.*

> *Your spouse or partner will thrive when he or she commits to the 3 Promises.*

> *Your friendships will strengthen through mutual commitments to the 3 Promises.*

> *Your business will grow from your commitment to the 3 Promises in every customer interaction.*

> *You'll benefit from your boss's commitment to creating a culture that encourages employees to live the 3 Promises at work.*

> *As an employer, you'll find that your people do their best work when they are committed to finding joy at work, using their strengths, and helping others.*

> *Your community will flourish when you and your neighbors strive to enjoy each day; live your passions professionally and personally; and give your time, energy, and resources to make your community friendlier, kinder, and more supportive.*

Robert Aliota, president of Carolina Seal, Inc., an engineered-products, services, and solutions company, had this to say after completing the 3 Promises Challenge: "On the third day, after completing my '3Ps' exercise, two things became clearer to me: First, how much of a positive impact we can each have on others at home and at work if we simply make a conscious effort to help people in some way each day, and how that can then become an unconscious habit over time. And second, just being aware of your gratitude for the impact you can have on others each day helps energize your mood and enhances your perspective on things happening in your life."

Reinforcement

AT THE END OF YOUR DAY, STOP FOR REFLECTION. IF YOU WANT TO ENSURE your own satisfaction with another day lived, revisit your promises each evening before you turn the page on the day. If you can, take the time to complete any unfinished promises you'd made for the day. Your purposeful actions—whatever their size and scope—will continue to breathe energy into your commitment to live a fulfilling life every day.

Laura Casellas, a leader in the field of teaching English as a second language, had this reflection after she completed the 3 Promises Challenge: "What a gift the 3 Promises Challenge was for me! I've been very overwhelmed lately and haven't balanced my various responsibilities in a way that satisfies me. In fact, I've been grumpy and irritable. I was feeling that something in my life was always getting the short end of the deal—either my work, my kids, downtime with my friends, or my commitment to staying healthy through exercising. These three days have gotten me back on track!"

Casellas continued, "I created joy, when, previously, I hadn't been able to find it every day. I am doing what I love by being a mom, making time to play tennis each week with my friends, and helping international students prepare for success in college. And I became intentional about making a difference—I found that changing my orientation, from "getting through my to-do list" to seeing what I'm doing as a way of making a difference at home and at work, changed my mindset and brought joy to these tasks. I've learned that I can focus on what's important when I follow the 3 Promises each and every day."

Making and fulfilling the 3 Promises every day will deepen your appreciation of life, nourish your relationships, and increase your contribution to others. You will discover for yourself the power you have to impact your life personally and professionally.

Once you convince yourself, through your own experience, that the 3 Promises fulfilled every day will lead you to a life of happiness, significance, and resilience, then return to your planner or journal and continue to record each day the traces of your personal and professional transformation. Bear witness to the good that is unfolding in your life. The key is to embrace the 3 Promises with your intention, your faith, and your action.

Share Ross is best known as the bassist in the 1980s all-female rock band, Vixen. Share is also a speaker, video production coach, personal development leader, on-air personality, and punk knitter. Here's Share talking about the 3 Promises Challenge, "I found myself paying attention to the choices I made throughout the day. Instead of mindlessly doing something, I became more conscious of my activities. Also, I discovered that I wanted to make a difference more than just once a day. This felt really good for me as it helped take the focus off my own internal struggles. By implementing The 3 Promises I felt calmer, I had a deeper sense of purpose, and I experienced more meaningful emotional connections. I was surprised to learn that I have a tendency to put off doing things I enjoy! Wow! I tend to feel a pull toward working a lot, and then that leads to an empty sort of feeling. So I'm definitely upping the enjoyment factor! Of course, the more I did things that I enjoyed . . . the easier it was to create what was needed for my work."

Savoring

ONE OF THE SWEETEST THINGS ABOUT LIVING THE 3 PROMISES EACH day is that you can extend and deepen your feeling of fulfillment through savoring.

When something good happens in our family, we do the "Happy Dance." With big smiles (it's impossible not to smile when you do what I'm about to share), this is what we say and do together:

Happy, Happy, Happy! (Timed to match each call of "Happy," we bounce up and down with our arms stretched overhead.)

Uh, uh, uh! (We match each "uh" with a twist of our hips.)

We repeat the dance three times, and we end with a big call out: "Happy!"

My girls do it. Dawn does it. My parents do it. In our family, we celebrate and amplify our important achievements.

The social psychologist Fred Bryant, a pioneer in the research on savoring, has found in his studies that, "Being able to savor positive experiences can boost the frequency, intensity, and duration of positive emotions. That's what savoring is all about—becoming more mindful of joy in one's life. And over time, this enhanced experience of joy in turn may promote better physical health."

Replaying your successes in your thoughts throughout the day, and reflecting on them in your 3 Promises journal, injects additional energy into all the 3 Promises actions you've taken. What you might have previously taken for granted, you now appreciate.

A Reminder

SOMETIMES ALL THE ENCOURAGEMENT YOU NEED TO FULFILL EACH OF your 3 Promises is a reminder. Sean Doyle, a senior attorney at a Fortune 500 health-care company, human rights lawyer, writer, and university instructor, talked about what he did during the 3 Promises Challenge to help him remember to integrate the 3 Promises into his day; "I printed out the 3 Promises card before bed, and I put it with my wallet and keys where I would see it the next morning. I then had it with me at work in my portfolio, so I would see it throughout the day. Having the reminder helped me, particularly when I was starting out."

Doyle continued, "The idea of seeing and reviewing the promises helps us to develop positive habits. And the name 'Promises' is great. As I was getting ready for bed, I saw the card again, and it reminded me of the commitment I had made. I fulfilled it, and I felt good following through."

If you would like your own 3 Promises card, you can print one out at www.The3Promises.com

The 3 Promises Planner–Journal

YOU DO NOT NEED A PLANNER OR A JOURNAL TO LIVE THE 3 PROMISES EVERY day. What's key is that you take actions that fulfill your promises. However, if you're like me and appreciate a little structure, you might consider using a 3 Promises Planner-Journal. I carry mine wherever I go. It's how I plan, how I record, and how I appreciate a fulfilling day.

I begin each day by writing down in my Planner-Journal all the actions I'm going to take that day to fulfill each of the 3 Promises. I include the small things—get up early, drink tea, read the paper, listen to music, pray. I include the bigger things—give a speech, coach a client, draft a chapter, work on a project, talk to a customer. I make sure to account for all the steps I must take to move my projects ahead, meet my responsibilities, and achieve my goals.

Every day I dedicate a page in my Planner-Journal to each promise, and each page has two columns. I use the first column to record everything I plan to do that day, and I use the second column to write down what I complete, including unplanned actions that help me fulfill the 3 Promises. Then at the end of the day I have clear evidence of my fulfillment.

I view my personal and professional accountabilities through the 3 Promises lens. I craft my work so that it feels like I'm fulfilling one of the promises. By integrating my personal and professional life inside the 3 Promises, I create the experience of fulfillment throughout my day. The result is that I'm more joyful, I'm more engaged at work, and I'm more giving to others. I feel happier, and everyone around me benefits.

Life is better when lived in the light of fulfillment.

If you're interested in using a 3 Promises Planner-Journal, visit www.The3Promises.com.

Your Turn

Now, it's time. You have what you need to take the 3 Promises 3-Day Challenge. Have fun with it, and tell me how it goes at www.The3Promises.com.

The 3 Promises 3-Day Challenge

The 1st Promise: Find Joy Every Day

PLAN, FIND, CREATE, OR PARTICIPATE IN AT LEAST ONE ACTIVITY THAT brings you joy today. Write the activity down. Commit to it. Schedule it. Make it happen. Enjoy it! Do this for three days in a row.

PLANNED	FULFILLED
Day One	
Day Two	
Day Three	

The 2nd Promise: Do What You Love

DO SOMETHING TODAY THAT EXPRESSES WHAT YOU LOVE DOING professionally or personally. Think of what you want to be doing more of in your career or in your life (interests, passions, hobbies). Do something that uses your natural gifts, something that lights you up on the job, and something that brings out your best. Write the activity down. Commit to it. Schedule it. Get it done. Love it! Do this for three days in a row.

PLANNED	FULFILLED
Day One	
Day Two	
Day Three	

The 3 Promises 3-Day Challenge

The 3rd Promise: Make a Difference

HELP SOMEONE TODAY. GIVE YOUR TIME, ENERGY, AND TALENT TO OTHERS. Do something that matters to another person. Write one activity down. Commit to it. Schedule it. Get it done. Make a Difference! Do this for three days in a row.

PLANNED	FULFILLED
Day One	
Day Two	
Day Three	

Daily Notes and Reflections

WRITE DOWN YOUR REFLECTIONS, IDEAS, OPPORTUNITIES, ACHIEVEMENTS, insights, and feelings of gratitude based on your experience fulfilling the 3 Promises each day. What new ways can you Find Joy, Do What You Love, and Make a Difference? What did you learn about yourself today? What did you learn about the impact you had on others?

Day One

Day Two

Day Three

The 3 Promises Fulfilled in Fifteen to Thirty Minutes

I BELIEVE YOU NEED ONLY FIFTEEN TO THIRTY MINUTES A DAY TO FULFILL your 3 Promises.

I've purposely placed this claim near the end of the book because I don't want a time frame to limit or to distract you, but I do want you to know that the time required to achieve daily feelings of happiness and fulfillment is less than you might think.

No matter what your role is or how many commitments you may have over the course of the day, I believe you'll be able to find some discretionary time—at least five to ten minutes for each promise—to find joy, use your strengths, and help others. Research tells us that even brief periods of living the 3 Promises add up to something meaningful. Miraculously, you will also find that once you commit a few minutes to the 3 Promises every day, you'll actually find more time to spend on what's important.

Here are just a few examples of things that might help get you started on your own 3 Promises Plan.

First Promise: Find Joy Every Day

Savor your coffee or tea

Read the paper

Stop in at your local café

Eat breakfast with your family

Share a snack with a coworker

Listen to music

Pray

Walk

Meditate

Call a friend

Watch birds

Practice yoga

Stretch

Take a hot shower or bath

Write in a journal

Put the house in order

Plan your meals

Look at pictures

Look at objects that have meaning in your life

Watch TV

Cuddle with a loved one

Put on your pajamas

Read before bed

Throw snowballs

Hug and kiss your family

Walk home from the bus stop with your child, hand in hand

Talk to God

Appreciate your strengths

Recall your achievements

Have a stimulating conversation

Sing along with your favorite songs

Star gaze

Watch your children play

Read funny social media posts

Dance

Watch the sunrise or sunset

Remember the support you have

Take a power nap

Drink your favorite beverage

Watch an uplifting video

Read something inspirational

Enjoy a snack

Play a video game

Walk or play with your dog, cat, or other pets

Second Promise: Do What You Love

Write an idea for an article

Read a few pages of a book that inspires you

Look over a speech you'll be giving soon

Craft part of your business plan

Research a new method for improving your business

Practice a song you really want to sing well

Dance a dance that excites you

Promote a product, service, or idea

Analyze research or financial data

Study something new

Brainstorm new ideas

Do something challenging

Do something you do naturally well

Write a poem

Write a blog post

Take a photograph

Cook

Draw

Paint

Play games online

Speak another language

Play musical instruments

Play sports

Engage your hobby

Third Promise: Make a Difference

Help a loved one

Check in on a friend

Say thank you

Pray for someone

Mentor someone

Introduce someone

Welcome people

Include people

Post something positive about someone

Make your family laugh in the morning

Read to your children at night

Write a thank-you note

Help with homework

Run your partner's errand

Hug someone

Provide advice

Offer encouragement

Give a massage

Do a quick favor

Plant a flower

Make a financial contribution

Let cars pass in front of you

Hold the door for people

Wake a family member joyfully

Tuck someone into bed

Arrive early

Do a chore for someone

APPRECIATE THE POWER OF TURNING YOUR ENERGY EVERY DAY TO WHATEVER it is that brings you joy, expresses your natural gifts, and allows you to contribute to others. Make a commitment to yourself that you will set aside at least five to ten minutes for each promise. The positive impact of doing so will touch everything and everyone in your life.

Total 3 Promises Activities

GOING ON DATES WITH DAWN AND EACH OF MY DAUGHTERS IS WHAT I CALL a Total 3 Promises activity: an activity that allows me to fulfill all three promises at one time. For me it's fun to go out with Dawn and my daughters (Find Joy), talk to them (Do What You Love), and show them how much I love them with my respect, interest, and attention (Make a Difference).

Find out what your own Total 3 Promises activities are. You'll feel the power of those activities each time you do them.

Paula Bloom, a nationally known psychologist and frequent television commentator, crafted a Total 3 Promises activity during her 3 Promises 3-Day Challenge. She said, "The benefit of even just the imagining/planning of 3 Promises activities is huge. It got me rethinking my day. So, for example—I knew a friend (not a particularly close friend) was struggling with some things. I might have just given her a hug after the meeting we both attend, but because of the 3 Promises Challenge, I decided to reach out to her the night before and ask her to meet for coffee after the meeting. Had it not been for the challenge, I may not have made this gesture at this particular time."

Bloom continued, "It felt good to reach out to plan the coffee date, and then, the next day I had the coffee date. Two days of bang for my one 'buck.' But even more interesting was how one activity touched all 3 Promises. I enjoyed making the date, and I enjoyed our time in the café. I love helping people, so I felt I was engaging my strengths during our chat, and I was able to help my friend."

Demands on Your Time

FOR SO MANY OF US, EACH DAY CARRIES A LOAD OF RESPONSIBILITIES THAT must be honored and met—so many demands are made on our time, energy, and attention by other people. The 3 Promises are a reminder that we must give ourselves the power and freedom to make requests of ourselves as well, and to prioritize them at least as much as the requests of others. Honoring the 3 Promises is a daily responsibility to ourselves. We are worthy of the rewards that come from making and honoring the 3 Promises.

Remember, practicing the 3 Promises every day is going to take your life in a new direction. You will awaken to an abundance of joy, opportunities to express your talents through your work, and the privilege to contribute to the fulfillment of others.

Missing a Promise

BUT, WHAT HAPPENS WHEN YOU DON'T FULFILL A PROMISE ONE DAY? Breakdowns happen. Things get in the way. Circumstances arise. The best remedy—rather than beating yourself up and feeling like you've failed—is to acknowledge that you have work to do to fulfill a promise, that you respect the impact your broken promise has on yourself and others, and that you need to get into action to fulfill your promise.

You'll live a happier and more meaningful life when you hold yourself accountable to these promises, and you'll have an enormously positive impact on all the people you care about: your family, friends, and coworkers.

Remember, you're up against the constant demands and challenges of daily living when you undertake the 3 Promises. Some days you may feel stressed by too many deadlines and the need to deal with other priorities. You'll feel pressed to meet other commitments at work and at home. It's easy to put off finding joy in your days, using your gifts, and helping others when you're in the midst of a busy life. Below are a few of my own experiences with the 3-day challenge.

Finding My Joy Every Day

DURING ONE PARTICULARLY STRESSFUL PERIOD LAST YEAR, I HAD PLANS to meet Dawn and our girls on vacation at Disney World. I was flying in from another city, and I was meeting them at the Orlando airport. I had just come from a number of intense meetings, and I was in a serious mood. I was struggling to switch gears from writing and speaking deadlines to theme park rides. That's when a close friend reminded me of the First Promise to Find Joy. He told me to meet my work responsibilities, but he encouraged me to become "fun Dad" by the time I arrived at the airport. My friend's guidance was the poke I needed to fulfill the promise. I got my work done, and I arrived smiling with activities planned that would bring joy to all of us.

Doing What I Love

I AM JUST AS LIKELY TO WASTE FIFTEEN MINUTES IN MY DAY AS ANYONE ELSE. It's easy to do and easy to think, whether you're conscious of it or not, that you don't have enough time in the day to do something meaningful. What I've realized, in making the 3 Promises, is that this is not true. You can fulfill a promise in five to ten minutes—and considering how many of these in-between times we have in our lives, you can make a big difference if you put them to work.

Here's an example from my own life. The best writers say that to be a good writer you have to read a lot. So, I often use those in-between times to read, sketch out stories, or call a colleague to swap some ideas. My practice of reading inspirational works and writing first thing in the morning assures me of fulfilling the Second Promise every day.

When you look back to the second part of the book, "Do What You Love: The Second Promise," you'll be reminded of the many ways you can break down your big goals into tasks that can be accomplished in small chunks of time. Every day you can make progress in doing more of the work you love.

Making a Difference

WHEN THERE IS SOMETHING I DON'T WANT TO DO, BUT I KNOW IT HAS meaning, I try to make it my "give." I take it out of the "I don't feel like doing it" column and put it into the "Make a Difference" column. I focus on the difference it will make for someone else. I try not to let personal feelings get in the way of making a difference when and where I can. Others benefit as a result of my contribution, and so do I.

When you're feeling down or anxious, retreating into self-absorption is not the answer. This is the time to "up your give." Focus outward on the difference you can make for someone. And don't worry about having enough ideas. Just think of everyone in your life. Think about what they care about. Think about what they like. Focus on what's meaningful to them, and you'll have a list of things to choose from. You'll have plenty you can do to brighten or ease the day of a coworker, a loved one, or a friend.

The richness that comes from giving to others has a multiplying effect that's hard to measure. The number of people who are ultimately impacted by your contribution may not be known for years. The key is to give meaningfully today. You will live in the glow of making a difference in someone else's life.

You've Done It!

YOU'VE NOW TAKEN THE 3 PROMISES 3-DAY CHALLENGE AND BROUGHT THE 3 Promises into your life. You've experienced the good that happens when you make a commitment every day to Find Joy, Do What You Love, and Make a Difference. You've seen the positive impact the promises have on your life and the lives of the people you touch. And all of this happened in three days.

Now it's time to build on what you've started—and live the fulfilling life you were meant to live, every day.

Take The 3 Promises Pledge

IMAGINE A WORLD THAT EMBRACED AND ENCOURAGED US TO LIVE FULFILLING lives. How beautiful it would be if all of us—our families, friends, co-workers, and neighbors—felt the passion, power, and peace of mind that comes with living the 3 Promises every day.

Take a stand and let people know your commitment to Finding Joy Every Day, Doing What You Love, and Making a Difference. Join thousands of people around the world. Take the 3 Promises Pledge and share it with others. Give them a gift of a new way of living, a daily path to fulfillment.

Visit www.the3promises.com to take the 3 Promises Pledge now.

PART 5

Amplify
Your Positive Impact

"A life is not important except in the impact it has on other lives."
—Jackie Robinson

WE NOW KNOW THE POWER OF THE 3 PROMISES TO INCREASE OUR happiness and fulfillment, and we can see the positive impact we have on others when we fulfill them. You can build a powerful identity when you approach life through the lens of the 3 Promises.

However, you can also expand the impact of the 3 Promises to the lives of your loved ones, friends, and coworkers. You can encourage them to find out how they bring joy to their own lives each day, do what they love, and make a difference in the world. By having what I call "3 Promises Conversations" with them, you'll discover what truly fulfills them and how you can support their efforts to achieve each of the 3 Promises.

You'll find that when you choose to live in what I call the "Promise Cycle," not the "Garbage Cycle," you will be able to contribute your positive energy more broadly to everyone around you. You'll be empowered to shift your focus from the things that annoy and frustrate you toward those that empower and energize you.

The 3 Promises Conversations

THE 3 PROMISES ALSO GIVE US THE OPPORTUNITY TO LEARN MORE ABOUT each other and better understand how to positively impact the people we value and care about by having 3 Promises Conversations at home and at work. If you're in a relationship, interview your partner. If you're a mom or dad, interview your children. If you're a boss, interview your employees. If you're a teacher, interview your students.

What will happen as a result? You'll know how to trigger their joy. You'll better know what motivates them. You'll know what type of recognition is meaningful to them. You'll know how to help them use their natural gifts personally and professionally. You'll know how to help them make a difference at home and at work.

3 Promises Conversations with Family

THE ANSWERS TO THREE SIMPLE QUESTIONS AMAZED ME WHEN I TRIED them myself in conversations with Dawn and my girls: They gave me great insight into how I can inspire and support the most important people in my life. Here are the three questions:

What brings joy to your life?

What do you love to do (what expresses your passion, interests, and strengths)?

How do you like to make a difference in the world?

I've been married to Dawn for fifteen years, and I learned even more about her when we talked about the 3 Promises over a quiet dinner. I have a deeper respect and appreciation for how much she enjoys being a mom and what brings her joy, how she likes to use her natural gifts, and how she prefers to make a difference. Among the many things she shared with me, Dawn told me how much she enjoys her quiet time before everyone wakes up in the morning, how much it means to her that we honor her schedule and routines during the week, and how much she enjoys leading Parent-Teacher Association projects at the school. Then, Dawn asked me the 3 Promises questions, and she learned more about me, too. Since our dinner, we have been more attentive and supportive of what brings us joy, what brings out our strengths, and what gives us meaning. If you're married or dating, I recommend you have this meaningful, enjoyable, and sometimes surprising, conversation.

I also talked to my ten- and eleven-year-old girls about their 3 Promises. I took each of them on a separate little date to our local café. I asked the 3 Promises questions, and I found out a lot about them—more than I even expected. My ten-year-old, Ariela, told me how much she loves to be with friends, to laugh, to hug—she said we all need fifteen hugs a day to be happy—and to read at night with Mami (Dawn) and me. Ariela talked about the things she loves to do—dancing, school, art, basketball, editing, and acting—all the things that bring out different aspects of her personality and that are important to her. Ariela also related how she likes to help her classmates in school. One story she shared was about a student who thanked her in front of the class for helping her make new friends. I congratulated Ariela, and I told her how everyone appreciates her kindness and compassion. Then, I shared with her a text that Mami received from a parent of a student in her class. The text read, "I wanted to let you know that my daughter was really upset about an earring she lost today, and Ariela was a great friend during the whole ordeal. I thought you'd like to know that she rocks even when you aren't looking."

My eleven-year-old, Eliana, told me during our conversation that she enjoys playing with friends, trying new things, working on arts and crafts, and reading with us at night (Dawn and I have read to our daughters before bedtime almost every night since they were born). Eliana loves singing, dancing, school, computers, after-school clubs, cooking, and basketball. She talked about how important it is for her to be involved in lots of activities because everything is interesting to her. Eliana reminded me of a recent tour we took of a middle school. On one of the tour stops, we visited the broadcast booth of the school news team in time to watch their program live. As we were watching the students produce and deliver the show, one of the students panicked because she couldn't get a video to run on cue. Desperate for help, she called out to a classmate who was working on another part of the broadcast. The other student ran over, and with some quick typing and toggling, she was able to get the video rolling. And she offered her assistance calmly and kindly.

During our 3 Promises conversation, Eliana asked me, "Do you remember when that girl fixed the problem?"

"I sure do," I said.

"I want to be that girl—the girl people call for help," Eliana said.

It was wonderful hearing how each of my daughters expressed herself. I loved how animated they became when they talked about each of the 3 Promises. These conversations are so easy to have—there are only three questions to ask—and yet they reach deep down and reveal so much.

Helping Your Loved Ones

THE BEAUTY OF THE 3 PROMISES CONVERSATION IS THAT ONCE YOU KNOW what brings joy to your loved ones, you can help them experience it and avoid doing things that will detract from their experience of joy. Once you know what your loved ones love to do, you can look for opportunities that will call on their strengths, passions, and interests. And when you know how they like to make a difference, you can help them find activities that will allow them to contribute meaningfully to others. You can help your loved ones live a fulfilling life when you know how they like to fulfill the 3 Promises.

Raising Children

WE'VE ALL HEARD THE SAYING ABOUT RAISING CHILDREN, "IT'S NOT WHAT you say. It's what you do." What matters to children is how their parents act. Their example is what's important. How they approach life is observed. What they prioritize is noticed. That's when the 3 Promises have such a big impact.

When parents include the 3 Promises in their daily lives, they demonstrate to their children that they value experiencing joy, doing what they love, and making a difference. They show their children how to live a fulfilling life.

Parents can now say something more than, "I just want my child to be happy." They can say they want their children to be *fulfilled*. And living the 3 Promises every day is one powerful way to achieve fulfillment.

The 3 Promises Projects

LAST YEAR, I WAS HIT WITH THE REALIZATION THAT I WAS OVERWEIGHT, BY any measure, and it felt like it happened overnight. My clothes didn't fit. My belly pressed on my belt. My knees, hips, and back were sore. Exercise made me feel worse. My stamina for working long hours was diminished, and it didn't take much to tax my heart and lose my breath.

I knew I was in bad shape. I had tried to ease up on eating, but my efforts were short-lived. Something would interrupt my program and I would give up. I'd let myself off the hook with an excuse. My problem was snacking, portions, and sweets. If I had stopped at the delicious and healthy food Dawn cooked for our family, I would have been fine. It was all of my extracurricular eating that was the issue.

And here's what is sad. It had become a way of life. For the better part of three years I went up and down with my weight. Mostly up and never very far down. I ached. I tired easily. I avoided the mirror.

Then "that day" came. I realized I was settling for a lesser life. I was tired of the aches and pains, the shortness of breath, the way my pants fit, the reduced energy, and the puffy way I looked. I had had enough. I was living at partial power. That's when it hit me. What if I applied the 3 Promises to a project aimed at improving my health and getting my weight back to a comfortable place?

Health

THAT'S JUST WHAT I DID—I CALLED IT MY "VITALITY PROJECT." I PULLED OUT a sheet of paper and wrote down the 3 Promises. Under each one, I listed all of the ways that my Vitality Project would increase my ability to fulfill each promise every day. I started with all the things that would increase my joy if I committed to this path.

The First Promise: Find Joy Every Day

- Ache less.

- Look better.

- Be lighter on my feet.

- Feel more comfortable in my clothes.

- Have more clothes to choose from.

- Enjoy exercise more.

- Breathe more easily.

- Feel stronger.

- Feel proud of the way I was taking care of myself.

Next, I listed all of the benefits of doing more of what I love to do as a writer and a speaker:

The Second Promise: Do What You Love

- More energy to write.

- More creativity.

- More stamina during my speeches and seminars.

- More strength to handle the logistics and set-up of my training programs.

- Confidence to tackle other difficult projects.

- More zest and vitality for my corporate customers and coaching clients.

- Increase my attention span for learning.

- Demonstrate the power of The 3 Promises through my own example.

- Share my journey publicly to inspire others to take on their own vitality projects.

- Expand the possibilities in my life.

Finally, I listed all of the things I could do that would help me make a difference in the lives of my family, friends, and clients by making a success of my Vitality Project:

The Third Promise: Make A Difference

- Have more energy to give to Dawn, my daughters, and my parents.

- Be a more active and energetic coach of my daughters' sports teams as a result of my improved cardiovascular health.

- Be less likely to suffer an illness that would diminish my capacity to contribute to my family, friends, colleagues, and community.

- Increase the chances of being around a lot longer for everyone!

- Be a walking, breathing, living example of vitality and health for my daughters, who are at pivotal ages for making healthy food and fitness choices.

AFTER TAKING A LOOK AT MY NOTES, I REALIZED I HAD NO CHOICE BUT TO take action. I went to work, and came up with three simple goals: I would eat lots of vegetables, limit desserts, and avoid snacks after dinner.

Then I added two exercise goals: To start, I would engage in cardiovascular exercise every day for twenty minutes, then I would work up to thirty–forty minutes each day. I would also add ten more minutes of strength training every other day.

My last goal was to get more sleep. I aimed for seven hours a night.
Remember, everybody's different. Make sure to evaluate where you are when you start a Vitality Project, and come up with a health plan that works for you.

Going Public

AFTER MAKING MY LISTS I BEGAN TO REACH OUT FOR SUPPORT. I SHARED my plans with my family and friends, including regular posts on social media. Each Monday I would weigh in and report my results. I shared what worked and what I was working on. People began to encourage me publicly through social media, email, on the phone, and in person.

In her book, *The Myths of Happiness,* the psychologist Sonja Lyubomirsky cites research that shows how helpful it can be to tell others about your promises: "A University of Scranton study found that people who made public New Year's resolutions were a remarkable *ten times more likely* to succeed at their goal (for example, quitting smoking, improving their relationships, becoming a vegetarian, and so on) than those who had not."

I asked everyone for healthy eating ideas and exercise strategies. I invited people to join me on their own Vitality Projects, and many did.

Then I took on a Promise Partner—someone who would encourage and hold me accountable. Every morning we would text a status report to each other on how we had done the day before, on exercise, eating, and sleep. We celebrated our successes and recommitted if we had fallen short. Slipping along the way was not the issue—that's part of life. It was getting back on track with each other's encouragement and reminders of the bigger picture that mattered most.

Each week I reviewed what I had written about my Vitality Project and how it would help me to fulfill the 3 Promises. I kept reminding myself that the choices I was making to forego late night snacks, eat fewer desserts, go to bed earlier, and spend more time exercising were significantly contributing to my fulfillment.

And here's what happened at the end of my project: I got into a healthy weight range, my waist dropped a few sizes, my clothes fit better, my stamina to write and speak increased, I had more energy to help others, and my aches and pains decreased.

Equally encouraging to me was the fact that I had lost weight nearly every week during a period that included Mother's Day brunch, my birthday party, Father's Day dinner, my older daughter's eleventh birthday, and a week-long vacation. On top of all this, I was still on the road speaking and attending conferences. In the past, any one of these events or trips would have been an excuse to get me off track and keep me from achieving my goals.

What about you? What would you like to improve in your life? What weighs most heavily on your mind or body? Where would you like to become more effective? What would help you to flourish more in the areas that matter most to you?

Make your 3 Promises Project one that will thrill you if you succeed. Start it today.

Find joy in it. Do more of what you love because of it. Make a bigger difference as a result of it.

Get it done, and increase your fulfillment.

Your 3 Promises Identity

YOU CAN TAKE ON A NEW IDENTITY OVERNIGHT WHEN YOU BEGIN LIVING the 3 Promises. You might think it will take time before your embrace of the 3 Promises will be noticed by others. The opposite is true. You'll begin to see almost immediately how differently people respond to you.

I once attended a conference where I was completely blending in. I was making little effort to extend myself. I wasn't throwing myself fully into learning, and I was holding back on what I was sharing with others. I was doing little to add to the experience of anyone else, and as a result, I wasn't leaving much of an impression on anyone. And, because of my minimal engagement, I was not surprised by the lack of interest others had in me during our partner and group exercises. The conference was two and a half days long, and I moved through the first two days of the event in this way.

Homework

THE NIGHT BEFORE THE LAST DAY OF THE CONFERENCE, WE WERE GIVEN a homework assignment. I had been given one the night before, but I had completed the bare minimum. I gave little to what was asked, and the next day it showed. My contribution to others was minimal.

Then, on the last night, as I began to do the homework, something triggered me to think about the 3 Promises; it probably was my recognition of how much I was holding back and how I was not feeling good about it.

I wasn't having fun. I wasn't using my gifts, and I wasn't helping anyone else. So, I decided to take on my homework through the 3 Promises filter.

I started with a focus on joy. I made a cup of hot tea—which I love—and turned on my favorite music for reading and writing (our homework required both). My emotional state began to change. Then, I thought to engage my love of reading and writing, and to go above and beyond the request of the assignment, and do additional research on the assigned subject. I would strive to achieve a deeper perspective on what we were studying. I then typed up my homework, adding what I had discovered in my research. I was intent on making a greater contribution to the discussion groups the next morning.

The Shift

THE NEXT DAY, I WAS BACK AT THE CONFERENCE SITTING IN A NEWLY formed discussion group (the groups changed every day). The conference leader requested that we begin sharing the insights we had gleaned from doing the homework. We went around the circle, and I was set to go last. When it was my turn, I pulled out my notes and began to share my ideas and references to a couple articles that I had found in my research.

As I was speaking, I realized a shift was occurring in the way people were responding to me. First, everyone was listening intently. Second, a few members of the group commented on the additional research I had done and asked me where they could find the information I had uncovered. Third, during a five-minute break following our discussion, two people came up to me and handed me their business cards. They asked for mine and said that they would like to remain in contact. And one of the participants pulled me to the side and said how impressed he was with my analysis of the subject we were studying. He was equally impressed with the effort I had put into the homework. Then, he asked me if I would have lunch with him at the company he owned.

The change in how people were responding to me was overwhelming. People viewed me in a new way. They saw me as deserving of their attention, and they wanted to associate with me. My identity had changed.

That morning I showed up differently. My energy was positive, my strengths were engaged, and my desire to contribute to the group was evident. I was living the 3 Promises.

The impact on me was twofold. I learned a lot more from the way I applied myself to the homework, and as a result, I felt the conference was more valuable to me. I then recognized the different imprint I had made on others by my participating in the conference through the 3 Promises frame. I appeared to the group as someone who enjoys the work, who takes on work fully, and who has a lot to contribute.

What a difference.

I set a new standard for myself. I had proof I could meet it, and I could live inside this new identity with joy, passion, and meaning.

You'll have the same experience as you begin living the 3 Promises. Take notice of how much more attractive you are to people, how much more you can help others, and how many more opportunities begin to show up in your life.

The Promise Cycle
and the
Garbage Cycle

I BELIEVE THERE ARE TWO CYCLES OF ENERGY OPERATING IN THE WORLD AT all times: the "Garbage Cycle" and the "Promise Cycle."

We all choose moment to moment which cycle we live in.

As I describe in my book, *The Law of the Garbage Truck*, the Garbage Cycle is fueled when we focus on the negative, act impatiently, harbor grudges, complain often, speak ill of others, and wallow in pessimism. When you're in the Garbage Cycle, you feel pressured, burdened, and stressed. You feel self-righteous and believe that everything that is wrong with the world lies beyond your control. Someone else is always at fault. Something else is always the problem.

On the other hand, the Promise Cycle is fueled when you Find Joy Every Day, Do What You Love, and Make a Difference. When you focus on the good things in life, express gratitude, have faith, are kind, show love, and share your optimism with others, you are living in the Promise Cycle.

The Law of the Garbage Truck is the key to avoiding the Garbage Cycle; making and honoring the 3 Promises is the key to living in the Promise Cycle.

When you stop accepting emotional garbage, creating it, and dumping it, you immediately step out of the Garbage Cycle and into the Promise Cycle.

When you make and honor the 3 Promises each day, you live freely and happily in the Promise Cycle.

And when someone's bad behavior is about to thrust you into the Garbage Cycle, you need only to follow The Law of the Garbage Truck and return to the Promise Cycle, where you can resume focusing on what's joyful, engaging, and meaningful.

The psychologist Robert Emmons reminds us of this in his book *Gratitude Works*: "Because you can't be grateful and negative at the same time, gratitude counteracts feelings of envy, anger, greed, and other states harmful to happiness."

You have the freedom to choose where to place your attention in life. You are invited every day to live either in the Promise Cycle or the Garbage Cycle. Powerful forces may pull you in both directions, but it is up to you to decide which invitation you'll accept.

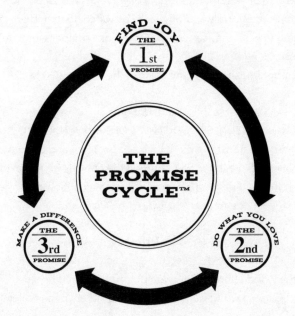

Which Invitation Are You Extending?

DECIDING WHICH INVITATION TO ACCEPT—THE GARBAGE CYCLE OR THE Promise Cycle—will determine your level of fulfillment. That we know. Deciding which invitation you will extend to others will influence their fulfillment. That's something to take seriously.

If what you say and do to others lessens their joy, diminishes their strengths, or makes them feel as though they're not making a difference, you'll know that you're drawing them into the Garbage Cycle. If your words and actions leave others feeling joyful in spirit, confident in their strengths, and proud of their giving, you're leading them into the Promise Cycle.

It takes courage to honestly assess the imprint we leave on others. It's easy to dismiss our bad behavior and unsupportive words when we're tired, sick, hurried, or stressed. It's harder to take responsibility for our words and actions.

If we want our relationships at home, at work, and in our communities to thrive, we must be conscious of the impact our conversations and actions have on others throughout the day. We must observe how people respond to us emotionally and physically by watching their body language and listening to what they say. We want to evoke people's joy, strengths, and purpose.

Remember, we all are worthy of life in the Promise Cycle.

Your Impact

THE INTERCONNECTEDNESS OF OUR LIVES OPENS A WINDOW TO TRANSFORM the world. We can transform more than our personal and professional relationships; we have the power, through the choices we make, to increase kindness, hope, and peace in the world. Just think of how many people are impacted by your commitment to living the 3 Promises.

The Urgency

THERE IS NO TIME TO WASTE.

Can the world afford to have you put off the benefits of your fulfillment? Can the world wait for you to help others become fulfilled, too?

We need your best now. And what greater gift could you give to the rest of us than your joy, talents, and giving?

It's time to stop hiding your light "in a bushel basket," as my grandmother used to tell me.

Bringing The 3 Promises to Work

"To find joy in work is to discover the fountain of youth."

Pearl S. Buck

YOU KNOW THAT LIFE IS BETTER—AND WORK IS BETTER—WHEN IT IS LIVED in the light of fulfillment. When you radiate joy, use your natural strengths, and help others, you transform the workplace every day. And when you help activate the 3 Promises in your colleagues, you help increase their joy, help them do more of what they love, and help them make a difference. The most immediate contribution you can make to your team is living The 3 Promises and activating them in others.

Remember, your manager has an important role to play in your fulfillment at work, but your role is equally significant. You are co-responsible with your manager—and your teammates—for creating a positive, supportive, and results-driven work environment.

The 3 Promises Shares

THE EASIEST WAY TO LEARN HOW YOU AND YOUR TEAMMATES CAN ACHIEVE fulfillment at work is to identify and share the actions that will help each of you fulfill the 3 Promises.

Find Joy Every Day

BEGIN BY ASKING EVERYONE ON THE TEAM TO SHARE HOW THEY FIND JOY Every Day. You can do this formally, in a scheduled meeting, or you can do it over coffee—whatever works best for you and your team. Once the sharing begins, take notes. What people share is the key to their heart, mind, and spirit, which teaches you how to trigger joy in their workday— and that's important. Remember when people are experiencing positive emotion, they're more kind, generous, and helpful. "They also have broader attention, greater working memory, enhanced verbal fluency, and increased openness to information," writes Chris Peterson in *A Primer in Positive Psychology*. Studies of work teams experiencing frequent positive emotion have also outperformed their peers "on three distinct business indicators: profitability, customer satisfaction ratings, and evaluations by superiors, peers, and subordinates", according to Barbara Fredrickson.

Do What You Love

NEXT, ASK EVERYONE TO TALK ABOUT THE SECOND PROMISE, DO WHAT YOU Love. Find out what they enjoy doing at work. Do they love to Research? Market? Sell? Present? Interview? Write? Analyze? Create? Plan? Administer? Organize? Celebrate? Recognize? Motivate? Study? Coordinate? Manage? Speak? Train? Their answers will let you know what lights them up in their job and career. When you are able to engage the interests of your teammates, you can more thoughtfully involve them in your projects based on their passions, and you can suggest creative job sharing ideas, too. And when employees craft their jobs to include more of what they love to do—while still meeting their responsibilities—their satisfaction, commitment, attachment to the job, engagement, and performance increases.

The key to fulfilling the Second Promise is to make the most of the job you currently have, and to take incremental steps every day toward doing even more of what you love. That might mean taking advantage of expanded opportunities in your current job, accepting a temporary assignment, or taking on a new role.

We also know that when you call upon people's strengths, you amplify them. In *The Strengths Book*, positive psychology researchers Alex Linley, Janet Willars, and Robert Biswas-Diener report that "People who use their strengths are happier, more confident, have higher levels of self-esteem, have higher levels of energy and vitality, experience less stress, are more resilient, are more likely to achieve their goals, perform better at work, are more engaged at work, and are more effective at developing themselves and growing as individuals."

Make A Difference

FINALLY, ASK EVERYONE ON THE TEAM TO SHARE HOW THEY LIKE TO FULFILL the Third Promise—Make A Difference—at work. Find out how your teammates like to help others. This knowledge will enable you to recognize opportunities for your teammates to give in a meaningful way. In his research, Wharton Business school professor Adam Grant has discovered that "as people make voluntary decisions to help colleagues and customers beyond the scope of their jobs, they come to see themselves as organizational citizens." Teams can also play a giving role by agreeing to help another group in the company with a project, identify a charity to support with their time, money, and resources, or engage in a community-building activity. The psychologist Stephen Post found, in his research, that when employees volunteered through their workplace, seventy-five percent of them felt better about their employers as a result. When employees give of themselves, everyone benefits. "Givers," as Grant calls them, enjoy greater success at work, and contribute more to a company's revenue growth and profitability.

A Note About Your Manager

SOME PEOPLE WONDER WHAT THE BEST WAY IS TO GET ALONG WITH THEIR boss. This is an important issue because research indicates that the number one reason people leave their jobs is because they don't get along with their manager. Here's a quick guide to nourishing a relationship with your boss.

Make an effort to activate The 3 Promises in your boss. Help them find joy every day: What can you do that will activate their joy at work?

Help them do what they love every day: Look for the chance to call upon their strengths. Be on the lookout for opportunities where they can make a difference: There will be times when they can help you, your team, and your company. And be sure to recognize them as they achieve each of the 3 Promises.

Furthermore, once you know your boss's strengths, you can take the initiative and offer to help them in areas where they're not as strong. President of the Canadian Positive Psychology Association Louisa Jewell recently told me, "I always like it when a member of my team says, 'Louisa, I know you hate this stuff, so leave it to me. I'm happy to do it.'"

The same guidance applies to a boss working with a difficult employee. Follow the same plan above, and you'll trigger the best in your employees.

Daily Action for Fulfillment

THE MOST IMPORTANT THING ABOUT THE DAILY ACTION THAT YOUR teammates choose is that it brings them joy every day; it should be something that allows them to do what they love, and enables them to make a difference. When people make the 3 Promises every day, they feel at peace and excited at the same time. They're at peace because they're living a fulfilled life now, instead of waiting for a day in the future to experience fulfillment. And they're excited because they are making progress towards their goal, and increasing the amount of time they are dedicating each day to doing what they love.

When teammates have the answers to what contributes to each other's fulfillment, they offer support, encouragement, and appreciation for each other. They will also discover common themes that cut across the organization. It's here that, as a team, they can create a work environment that inspires the fulfillment of the 3 Promises.

Keep It Simple

PEOPLE-DEVELOPMENT PROCESSES NEEDN'T BE COMPLEX. IN FACT, SIMPLE processes are more apt to promote adoption and usage than more complex processes. The more intricate the approach, the less likely it will be used over the long term. People are too busy to memorize and follow complicated processes. That's the beauty and power of the 3 Promises:

they are easy to integrate into all the important people-related activities in the company. You can ask candidates, during the hiring process, and employees, during new-hire orientation or quarterly performance check-ins and annual reviews, how they plan to fulfill the 3 Promises. When you do, you'll glean invaluable information about what brings them joy, what they love doing, and how they like to contribute to the team. Integrate the 3 Promises in your approach to customer care, and your employees will evoke joy in their customers, use their gifts in service of them, and view taking care of their customers as an opportunity to make a difference.

When you help company stakeholders find joy, do what they love, and make a difference, you strengthen your relationships with them. People are naturally drawn to people and companies that evoke in them the feeling and achievement of fulfillment.

So go put the 3 Promises to work in your business. You and your team will be glad, and so will your customers.

More Resources

FOR MORE RESOURCES AND INFORMATION TO HELP YOUR ORGANIZATION introduce, teach, and promote the 3 Promises, visit www.The3Promises.com

To bring David or his team to your organization to speak, train, or coach, visit: www.DavidPollay.com

References

PART ONE: Find Joy Every Day: The First Promise

Lyubomirsky, S. *The Myths of Happiness*. London: Penguin Press, 2013.

Chapter 1

Frederickson, B. *Positivity*. New York: Harmony, 2009.

Chapter 2

Csikszentmihalyi, M. *Finding Flow*. New York: Basic Books, 1997.

Chapter 3

Keltner, D., and Haidt, J. "Appreciation of Beauty." In *Character Strengths and Virtues*, ed. C. Peterson and M. Seligman. New York: Oxford University Press, 2004.

Newberg, A., and H. R. Waldman, *How God Changes Your Brain*. New York: Ballantine Books, 2009.

Smith, H. *The Religions of Man*. New York: Harper Collins, 1958.

Chapter 4

Associated Press, file. (2006, May 11). Heavyweight champ Floyd Patterson dead at 71. *Sun Sentinel*.

Chapter 6

Solomon, R.C. Foreword to The *Psychology of Gratitude,* ed. R.A. Emmons and M.E. McCullough, p. v–xi. New York: Oxford Press, 2004.

Bonhoeffer, D. *Letters and papers from prison* (E. Bethge, Ed.). New York: Macmillan, 1967.

Chapter 9

Fredrickson, B.L. *Positivity*. New York: Crown, 2009.

Chapter 10

Emmons, R. *Thanks! How the New Science of Gratitude Can Make You Happier*. New York: Houghton Mifflin Harcourt, 2007.

Chapter 12

Baumeister, R.F., E. Bratslavsky, C. Finkenauer, and K.D. Vohs. 2001. "Bad is stronger than good." *Review of General Psychology* (vol. 5): 323–70.

Chapter 16

Gottman, J.M., and J. DeClaire, *The Relationship Cure*. New York: Three Rivers Press, 2001.

Vaillant, G. *Aging Well*. New York: Little, Brown and Company, 2003.

Keltner, D. *Born to Be Good*. New York: W.W. Norton & Company, 2009.

Ruch, W. "Humor." In *Character Strengths and Virtues,* ed. C. Peterson and M. Seligman. New York: Oxford University Press, 2004.

Chapter 17

Rumi, Jalal al-Din. *The Essential Rumi*. Translated by Coleman Barks and John Moyne. New York: HarperOne, 2004.

Chapter 19

Seligman, M.E.P. Authentic Happiness: *Using the New Psychology to Realize Your Potential for Lasting Fulfillment*. New York: Free Press, 2002.

Chapter 27

Lopez, S. *Making Hope Happen*. New York: Atria Books, 2013.

McAdams, D. *The Stories We Live By*. New York: The Guilford Press, 1993.

Chapter 32

King, S. *On Writing*. New York: Pocket Books, 2000.

Chapter 39

Gottman, J.M., and N. Silver, *The Seven Principles for Making Marriage Work*. New York: Three Rivers Press, 1999. Chapter 43.

Chapter 41

Pollay, D. *The Law of the Garbage Truck*. New York: Sterling Publishing, 2010.

Chapter 45

Gable, S.L., H.T. Reis, E.A. Impett, and E.R. Asher. 2004. "What Do You Do When Things Go Right? The Intrapersonal and Interpersonal Benefits of Sharing Positive Events." *Journal of Personality and Social Psychology (87*, No.2): 228–245.

Chapter 46

Gottman, J.M., and J. DeClaire, *The Relationship Cure*. New York: Three Rivers Press, 2001.

Chapter 48

Peterson, C. *A Primer in Positive Psychology*. New York: Oxford University Press, 2006.

Chapter 50

Saltzman, D. *The Jester Has Lost His Jingle*. Palos Verdes Estates: The Jester Co., Inc., 1995

Chapter 53

Duhigg, C. *The Power of Habit*. New York: Random House, 2012.

Bryant, F., and J. Veroff, *Savoring: A New Model of Positive Experience*. Mahwah, N.J.: Lawrence Erlbaum Associates, Inc., Publishers, 2007.

Chapter 56

Lyubomirsky, S. *The Myths of Happiness*. London: Penguin Press, 2013.

Chapter 57

Emmons, R. *Thanks! How the New Science of Gratitude Can Make You Happier*. New York: Houghton Mifflin Harcourt, 2007.

Bringing the 3 Promises to work

Peterson, C. *A Primer in Positive Psychology*. New York: Oxford University Press, 2006.

Fredrickson, B.L. *Positivity*. New York: Crown, 2009.

Wrzesniewski, A. (2014). Presentation to the International Positive Psychology Association in the Positive Psychology Leaders Series: *Crafting Meaningful Work*.

Linley, A., Willars, J., and Biswas-Diener, R. *The Strengths Book*. United Kingdom: CAPP Press, 2010.

Grant, A. *Give and Take*. New York: Penguin Group, 2013.

Post, S. (2014). Presentation to the International Positive Psychology Association in the Positive Psychology Leaders Series: *Rx: It's Good to Be Good*.

Acknowledgments

MY THANKS BEGIN WITH MY FAMILY. MOM HAS BEEN MY FIRST-LINE EDITOR for my columns and my books. Working with her has been one of the supreme joys of my life. Mom has been a beacon of love for me, our family, and my friends. I'm grateful to my dad (aka, Big Lou) for his humor, encouragement, and confidence in me. Dad has always been my rock and my buddy.

Thank you to my wife, Dawn, for the joy she brings to my life. Her smile and spirit light me up, and everyone around her. Dawn supports me in every way, and she is an amazing mother to our girls. We are blessed with two wonderful daughters, Ariela and Eliana. They are kind, passionate, and giving. My girls inspire me to live The 3 Promises each day. Dawn's parents, Terry and Marcia Gano, are the best in-laws you could ask for. They're fun, loving, and supportive of me and our whole family. Finally, I'm grateful to my brother, Mike, for his friendship, love, and wisdom.

Thank you to my agent, Ivor Whitson. Ivor is one of the nicest men I have ever known, a great agent, and a good friend. Thanks to Ivor's wife and partner, Ronnie, for her creative input along the way. Jennifer Williams at Sterling Publishing has been a gift to me. Jennifer was the first to make the case at Sterling to acquire The 3 Promises and The Law of the Garbage Truck. She is the editor of both books. Jennifer makes everything I write stronger, and she is a joy in every way. Thanks also to former Sterling VP Editorial Michael Fragnito for championing The 3 Promises and The Law Of The Garbage Truck inside and outside of Sterling. Michael's support has been very important to the success of both books. The entire team at Sterling has been tremendous: Deborah Stack, Christine Heun, Lauren Cirigliano, David Ter-Avanesyan, Elizabeth Mihaltse, Marilyn Kretzer, Toula Ballas, Josh Mirvos, Rodman Neumann, Karen Menzie, Sari Lampert, and Theresa Thompson.

Thank you to Stephanie Gunning for her insightful and skilled editing of an early draft of The 3 Promises. Thanks to Katie Otis for bringing the spirit of The 3 Promises to life through her original cover design, and thanks to Nikki Smith-Morgan for her creative web design.

Thanks to everyone who gave feedback to early drafts of the book or The 3 Promises 3-Day Challenge: Dawn Pollay, Share Ross, Paula Bloom, Susan Pollay, Laura Casellas, Randy Salim, Brenda Richterkessing, Preston Lewis, Robert Aliota, Sean Doyle, Chris Abbott, Frank Mosca, Hayley Foster, Christine Alestra, Louisa Jewell, Margaret Greenberg, Ron Wilber, Caroline Miller, Steve Greenbaum, and Shari Roth. Thanks to Cindy Rold for her insight into the power of "yes." Thanks also to the readers of my syndicated columns and blog posts over the years. Many of the strategies, tools, and stories in this book were first shared with them. Thanks for the additional support provided by Robin Rubin, Yakov Smirnoff, Hallé Pollay, John Spannuth, Tracey Capers, David Schmidt, Becky Remmel, Rick Brandon, and Alberto Casellas. Thanks also to store managers Tiffany Clute, Mike Hoffacker, Ren Valdes, shift supervisor Kenny Franciscus, and their Starbucks partners for their encouragement as I edited the book in their store.

I'm grateful to my mentors, professors, and colleagues in the field of positive psychology. Their research, collaboration, and encouragement have infused my work: Martin Seligman, Christopher Peterson, James Pawelski, Karen Reivich, Ray Fowler, Ed Diener, Sonja Lyubomirsky, Stephen Post, Adam Grant, Robert Emmons, and Barbara Fredrickson.

Finally, thank you for reading *The 3 Promises*.

Better yet, thank you for living The 3 Promises.

Index

Note: Page numbers in italics indicate promise action steps.

About the Author

DAVID J. POLLAY, M.A.P.P., IS THE CREATOR AND AUTHOR OF THE international blockbuster, *The Law of the Garbage Truck®*, translated into twelve languages.

David is a leader in the field of Positive Psychology. He served as co-founding associate executive director of the International Positive Psychology Association. He has held leadership positions at Yahoo!, MasterCard, Global Payments, and AIESEC. David holds a master's degree of applied positive psychology (M.A.P.P.) from the University of Pennsylvania and a bachelor's degree in economics from Yale University.

He has been featured on ABC, NPR, Univision, and in *BusinessWeek SmallBiz Magazine*, the *Baltimore Sun*, *Business Digest*, the *Sun Sentinel*, the *Chicago Tribune*, the *Los Angeles Times*, and media worldwide. He has spoken to audiences around the world, and he was a featured speaker at TEDx Delray Beach. David lives in Florida with his wife, Dawn, and their two daughters.

Visit David online at davidpollay.com.

For information about The 3 Promises, visit the3promises.com.

The 3 Promises™ Pledge

Join Thousands of Others from Around the World
and Take The 3 Promises Pledge.

I will
Find joy every day.

I will
Do what I love.

I will
Make a difference.

I will live a fulfilling life
Today and every day.

Now, you've taken The Pledge.
It's time to share it with others.

www.The3Promises.com